Gender Issues, Sex Offenses, and Criminal Justice: Current Trends

Gender Issues, Sex Offenses, and Criminal Justice: Current Trends

Sol Chaneles, PhD
Editor

The Haworth Press
New York

Gender Issues, Sex Offenses, and Criminal Justice: Current Trends has also been published as *Journal of Offender Counseling, Services & Rehabilitation,* Volume 9, Numbers 1/2.

The Haworth Press, Inc., 28 East 22 Street, New York, NY 10010

Library of Congress Cataloging in Publication Data
Main entry under title:

Gender issues, sex offenses, and criminal justice.

Previously published in Journal of Offender counseling, services & rehabilitation, v. 9, no. 1/2.
Includes bibliographies.
Contents: Inmate sexual aggression / Peter L. Nacci, Thomas R. Kane—Gender disparity in the setting of bail / Frances P. Bernat—The female offender's adjustment to prison life / Faye E. Sultan. . . [et al.]—[etc.]
1. Prisoners—United States—Sexual behavior—Addresses, essays, lectures. 2. Homosexuality—United States—Addresses, essays, lectures. 3. Women prisoners—United States—Addresses, essays, lectures. 4. Prostitution—United States—Addresses, essays, lectures.
I. Chaneles, Sol.
HV8836.G46   1984   364.3'7   84-15830
ISBN 0-86656-357-1

Gender Issues, Sex Offenses, and Criminal Justice: Current Trends

Journal of Offender Counseling, Services & Rehabilitation
Volume 9, Numbers 1/2

CONTENTS

Preface

The perverse money economy in prison leads to inexpressible sexual perversity. The youngest, poorest inmates are frequently victims of rape. For money, prisoners allow themselves to become male prostitutes as they allow themselves to act as guinea pigs for drug-company experiments. Some inmates who are raped literally lose their minds, others attempt suicide. Some inflict wounds on themselves in order to be transferred to a hospital where there is less chance that they will have to be coerced into some new sexual humiliation. This is all done with the knowledge of prison personnel; many are paid for their complicity. The origin of the sexual aberations that pervade all our prisons for the very young as well as for adults is to be found in the organization of our prisons.

Prisoners are denied opportunities for sexual expression because of the nature of confinement rather than because a judge decrees that a sentenced person shall be subject to sexual denial and deprivation. No state or federal law has ever been passed requiring that as a condition of prison confinement a person shall be denied the right of sexual expression. If such a law were ever passed or a judge ever to deliver such a sentence, the action would be quickly declared unconstitutional. But such laws don't have to be proposed or considered by legislatures because sexual denial takes place automatically along with the many other deprivations that are not specified under law.

Criminally violent homosexuality is widespread in prisons and condoned by officialdom because it constitutes still another area of behavior for arbitrary control and exploitation by the establishment. Those who commit forced attacks bribe their keepers to overlook the rules; the victims must bribe their keepers for protection and possible reassignment of cells. If consensual homosexuality among prisoners were legal, the prison establishment would find ways to circumvent the law since voluntary consent about anything in prison is intolerable to the mind of the establishment. In 1971 the Canadian government enacted a law which permits acts of homosexuality

This article is adapted from the author's *The Open Prison,* NY: The Dial Press, 1973; and appears with the permission of the author.

among consenting adults when performed in private. But the law did not extend to prisons, and the justification was that prisons are not private places. The same laws have been passed in the United States, but the prison establishment leads the protest against making the protections of the law available to prisoners, arguing that homosexuality leads to a breakdown in discipline.

Any journalist can readily report numerous instances of homosexual rape and obligatory male prostitution in prisons, even in prisons located in the hearts of big cities and close to public awareness. But the stories, unless they are likely to embarrass a public official around election time, are not considered newsworthy.

In the absence of specific laws about sexual expression, some prison officials have set up private visiting rooms for prostitutes to provide sexual services to inmates who can pay the price. A percentage is paid to the officials. In some states, prisoners with means are allowed temporary freedom for as long as it takes to find a sexual partner. Occasionally, a reported escape of a prisoner is little more than a case of an inmate who fails to return to his cell on time after a sexual caper outside the walls. In the vicinity of some major state prisons, there are rows of brothels whose clients are primarily inmates who pay their keepers for the privilege of a brief outing to find sexual gratification.

In a growing number of prisons conjugal visiting is permitted. This practice involves provision of a bedroom and sufficient time for an inmate to preserve patterns of sexual intimacy with a spouse, a pattern that would normally have been terminated by a sentence. But conjugal visiting is reserved for prisoners who officialdom defines as "good"—if he is an especially "good" prisoner, his female visitor does not have to prove she is the inmate's spouse. Some communities condone sexual visitations; some are openly hostile; most are indifferent. It is the same kind of indifference expressed towards homosexual rape.

In many states that permit daytime release of prisoners for the purpose of finding and keeping a job, work-release practices involve little effort on the part of prison personnel to find jobs. For many inmates "work" release is little more than a thinly disguised excuse to find sexual partners. What is most to be criticized about this practice is not that it helps to reduce some of the tensions of prison life, but that it becomes an additional form of manipulation and control in the hands of prison officialdom.

One of the worst forms of official and corrupt exploitation of the sexual lives over the past decade of inmates has been described at the Holmesburg prison in Pennsylvania. The practices are not unique to that state. At Holmesburg, prison management successfully tied the sexual needs of inmates to the vicious money system in the prison. Inmates with money to pay guards are allowed their choice of sexual partners from the prison population. Inmates who serve as informers may also choose sex partners for either a private or gang rape. Reluctant inmates who refuse to comply with these arrangements are punished by prison staff with beatings or transfer to isolation. Enforcement of this sex-money economy is brought about by threat of mutilation or death; the torturers are either guards or prisoners. Victims know they can do little to prevent the dire consequences of resistance.

To assure access to money so that the economy may function smoothly, guards covertly arrange with drug companies to provide inmate subjects for testing new and dangerous drugs. Token amounts are paid to inmates, giving them the means to buy sex; larger amounts are paid to prison staff for their cooperation. Inmates are eager to participate in dangerous drug experiments, recognizing that they have been specially selected by their captors as good prospects for taking part and trustworthy in keeping quiet.

The sexual life of most people in western society is regulated, more or less, by community standards and levels of education. Society provides no assurances and few formal means for an individual to find that form or frequency of sexual expression that best corresponds to his personality or his need of intimate relationships whether homosexual or heterosexual. Young people, the elderly, the infirm and handicapped, and those who are confined to institutions are all especially vulnerable to sexual deprivation as a practical matter rather than as a result of formal codes of behavior. Very short people, unusually tall, bald, plain-looking, or very shy people probably have many complaints about sexual expression that are as valid as any other, but five thousand years of civilized society have not made the sexual lives of these people any better; whatever formal or informal rules for sexual conduct exist are honored more in the breach than the observance. The only type of sexual behavior that can and should be prevented by civilized society is forceful violation of one's sexual privacy—rape, whether homosexual or heterosexual.

Prisons have proven unable to deal meaningfully or effectively with sexual expression without resorting to jungle warfare. The only kinds of sexual expression permitted or encouraged by the prison establishment are those that enhance the establishment's power, at the same time fostering among inmates a cynical disregard for law, privacy, and individual dignity. The techniques of violence are needed to preserve the sex-money system; society's need to eliminate this source of violence far outweighs any type of benefits for the select few.

For as long as we continue to need prisons, prisoners should be allowed periodic leaves or furloughs, as a matter of right rather than as purchased favor or under the guise of an evasive work or educational release. Most of our present prison population pose no threat of violence in the community, and furloughs would allow them to find their own level in all facets of community life including sexual expression. Government intervention that permits sexual visitation only for married prisoners is highly discriminatory against those whose preferred form of sexual expression is homosexuality and is equally discriminatory against unmarried prisoners.

When, in 1970, the New York State legislature convened public hearings to consider the possibility of enacting laws to make conjugal visiting possible, legislators were deluged by protests. Paradoxically, neither religious, political, nor humanitarian groups made the protests; it was the wives of prisoners themselves. They complained vehemently that visits to their spouses that included the possibility of sexual relations was personally humiliating and grossly demeaned the emotional aspects of sexual expression. The proposed laws were promptly shelved.

But California, New Jersey, Texas, North Carolina, and many county-run prisons have, since 1968, set up cottages for inmate residence where prisoners may receive spouses or people to whom they are engaged to be married. Rules in these prisons are flexible, and to offset the expected complaints of homosexual inmates, officialdom is tolerant of homosexuality.

There are several big problems associated with prisons whose policies regarding sexual expression might be considered "flexible." First, these prisons, many set up as experiments, tend to receive from other prisons a very select group of inmates who in the opinion of prison officials are likely to comply with the prison administration's *ad hoc* rules regarding sexual conduct. The selection of inmates for these places is not based on what the community expects or demands or what laws expect or demand. Second, these prisons operate on the basis of arbitrary decisions made by officials.

Officials are free to abandon the "flexible" practices at will and in the prisons where selection is made for transfer of inmates to "flexible" settings, inmates tend to become even more docile and submissive in complying with the demands of their captors in order to receive favorable consideration. But since the practices of "flexible" prisons come very close to the largely unregulated behavior as regards sex in the free community, they should be made an integral part of prison life for most prisons for as long as we continue to find them necessary. And prisons will be necessary as long as violence continues to be a part of American life.

Candid recognition of the sexual rights of prisoners and allowing these rights to be pursued would not turn prisons and nearby communities into bordellos or produce mass sex orgies. The sex-money economy of prisons has accomplished this already and the recognition of inmates' sexual rights would swiftly end much of the horror of the current practices.

For spouses, sweethearts, common-law partners, and intimate friends who do not find visiting that includes sexual expression a demeaning experience, such visitation should be allowed. For those whose mode of sexual behavior is homosexual, homosexual relations should be permitted both among consenting prisoners as well as with homosexual partners from outside of prison. For those whose only means for finding sexual expression is through the payment of prostitutes, male or female, prostitutes should be allowed to practice their occupation—as in Nevada where prostitution is legal and regulated by health agencies, or as it is in those states and cities where laws against prostitution are not enforced but where efforts are made to prevent venereal disease. Prisoners allowed to work and paid decent wages for their work should be allowed, if they desire, to maintain a semblance of normal sexual expression—it is for most people too fundamental a need to be allowed to become a tool of official repression.

But what of those whose behavior is too violent? What of those who, notwithstanding "flexible" rules, are violent aggressors? What of their need to satisfy sexual urges and longing for intimate social contact? For those men and women for whom confinement is essential until they mature out of violence or until society understands violent behavior well enough to control and curb it, the answer is social isolation—but isolation not in the traditional prison meaning of solitary confinement in grim, airless cells with short rations, but social isolation without physical deprivation, where work and study may continue, where recreation and rest may continue, where the ability to communicate by writing is not impaired. For violent offenders social isolation is indispensable, but without infringement of basic rights or conveniences other than the right to intimate social contact and sexual expression with others.

Sol Chaneles, PhD

Gender Issues, Sex Offenses, and Criminal Justice: Current Trends

Inmate Sexual Aggression: Some Evolving Propositions, Empirical Findings, and Mitigating Counter-Forces

Peter L. Nacci
Thomas R. Kane

ABSTRACT. This report updates the U.S. Bureau of Prisons' (BOP) on-going investigation of inmate sexual aggression. Despite the fact that inmate populations are becoming more volatile (greater levels of violence are seen in commitment offenses—prisons are 29% beyond rated capacity) only about two sexual assaults occurred per month in 1983 in a system that confines 31,000 inmates. In previous reports, covering the time period between 1973 and 1977, the same sexual assault frequency was observed.

This report also contrasts some of the findings from the Federal study with results from other reports. For example, several major studies contend that racial conflict is a major motivating force behind sexual assaults, but the Federal study calls this interpretation into question.

Third, the paper discusses the Federal Bureau of Prisons' policy on homosexual activity and family visitation programs.

Finally, the paper describes some processes in corrections which will make prisons generally safer for all inmates including better inmate risk assessment procedures, accreditation, prison architectural advancements, and work by the National Institute of Corrections. Corrections officials are urged to consider using "rape kits," a systematic procedure for gathering and testing evidence from alleged assailants and victims of sexual assault.

Peter L. Nacci, PhD, is Chief of Research, U.S. Bureau of Prisons, and Thomas R. Kane, PhD, is Research Analyst, U.S. Bureau of Prisons, 320 First Street, N.W., Washington, D.C. 20534.

The opinions expressed in this paper are those of the authors and are not necessarily the policy or opinion of the Federal Bureau of Prisons.

1

INTRODUCTION

Six years ago the Federal Prison System began an extensive and long standing investigation of homosexuality and sex related aggression among male inmates. The study employed conventional survey/interview techniques; it was unique in part because: (1) it took into account perspectives of both inmates and correctional officers on controversial topics like sex and rape, (2) inmate interviewees were selected at random from a stratified sample of Federal prisons and jails; and (3) because interviews were conducted by a person who had served more than ten years in prison himself.[1] Now, with the study results well documented and widely circulated it is possible to place the studies' findings in a broader theoretical perspective. This paper has several purposes: it presents an overview of some major findings in the literature and emphasizes some of the major findings from the Federal study. There is a discussion on the rationale behind the study's focal objective—discovering means to control inmate sexual aggression and homosexual activity. The alternative position (sexual freedom) is not without supporters (including some corrections officials) as we have learned from our speaking engagements. The paper contains an update of the Federal Prison System's "archive"—the number of recorded acts of sex related aggression. The authors speculate about the future; they discuss some emerging administrative trends and suggest what the consequences may be.

SOME EVOLVING PROPOSITIONS ABOUT PRISONER SEXUAL BEHAVIOR AND SEXUAL AGGRESSION

There are few studies dealing with prisoner sexual behavior and sexual aggression. This paper is not an extensive review of the literature; readers should consult more detailed accounts by Lockwood (1980); Bartollas, Miller, and Dinitz (1974); Propper (1981), and Nacci and Kane, (1984).[2] For purposes here, it is valuable to

---

[1]An overview of the study was issued by the Federal Prison System in 1982, as part of a series of documents on prison research (see "Progress Reports", and also *Federal Probation*, 1983; 1984). A paper on the study is reprinted in Carter, Glaser and Wilkens, 1984.
[2]A reading list on inmate sexual aggression was prepared by Shore (1981). Propper's treatment of the topic is informative because she references many studies from Canada and Europe which are usually overlooked by American authors. Wooden and Parker (1982) is an

consider some select generalizations about male inmate sexual and aggressive behavior.[3]

A first proposition is that *sexual aggression in prison serves aggressive, more than sexual needs.* There is little disagreement about this; most researcher's and prison managers agree that men rape other men to gain status, power, and influence in the prison (cf. Lockwood, 1980). This position is also advanced as an explanation of the origins of heterosexual rape by Brownmiller (1975). Proposition one is a very important component in the accumulating body of evidence because it follows that, remedial "programs" designed to produce a cathartic like reduction of sexual energy as a way to eliminate sexual aggression would not succeed.

Proposition two is that *sexual aggression "appears" to be racially motivated.* Scacco (1975) developed a scholarly treatise on proposition two arguing that blacks redress years of subjugation by assaulting whites. In numerous reports (Davis, 1968; Lockwood, 1980; Nacci and Kane, 1984) blacks outnumber whites among assailant groups and whites are more prevalent amont target groups, thereby giving sexual assaults the appearance of being racially motivated. However, it is premature to accept racial hostilities as a major motivating force; that whites are more likely to be victimized does not establish that they were selected because of their whiteness rather than because of their weakness. Even in prisons where racial tensions were minimal, the same racial proportions would be likely to occur.

Proposition three is that *sexual aggression in prison can be controlled.* Although there may be some disagreement about how to control sexual assaults, most agree that sexual assaults can be controlled through better inmate classification (assignment to living quarters and prisons), better surveillance, improved living conditions, or by programs that permit inmates to release sexual tensions.

Proposition four is that *sexual assaults in prisons are carried out by a deviant subpopulation.* The fact is that most inmates are free from interpersonal conflicts while they are in prison. Classic studies of subcultures from which prisoners are drawn reveal that the bulk

---

account of sexual aggression among inmates in the California system which includes a discussion about officer's opinions about inmate sexual activities.

[3]These are provided as a backdrop for some major findings from the Federal study. In the Government's report, hundreds of findings are reported; the meaning and importance of major findings may have been obscured.

of criminal activity is conducted by a small minority of individuals (Wolfgang and Ferricuti, 1967). Many accounts of prison rapes suggest that the same pattern exists. The proposition is best evidenced in the juvenile population studied by Bartollas et al. (1974); inmates high on the prison "exploitation hierarchy" endlessly victimized weaker inmates.

Propositions five to seven relate to consensual prison homosexual activity. Proposition five is that *homosexual activity in prison is dangerous, destructive, and leads to violence.* This is the most controversial proposition because it is the premise for the conclusion that sexual behavior should be controlled. It is supported by actuarial investigations by Sylvester, Reed, and Nelson (1977), and by Toch (1965), and it is endorsed by many corrections officials. Challenges to the proposition are advanced: (1) on Freud's behalf substantively in the name of the catharsis hypothesis (on grounds that release from deprivation-produced frustration would quiet restive inmates); and (2) by supporters of greater sexual freedom. However, the catharsis idea is discredited in the scientific literature and moral issues aside (for the moment), the authors favor greater control and explain why later.

Proposition six is that *homosexual activity is most prevalent in long-term facilities.* This obvious and seemingly unimportant statement is neither unimportant nor without a plausible competing alternative hypothesis. Incidence should be proportional to opportunity one could argue. However, long-term places of confinement are particularly devoid of the cues normally associated with sexual activity and hence one could expect "Bastilles" to diminish inmates' sexual desires. The preponderance of evidence supports the proposition (cf. Nacci and Kane, 1984). The importance of this whole matter revolves around our need to locate the phenomenon, study its pervasiveness, and establish programs where needed.

Proposition seven is that *men who participate in sex while in prison are not judged "homosexual" by peers if they perform male behaviors.* Like everyone else, inmates make causal judgments about why people do what they do. If inmates are not "free" to do otherwise (because of lack of women or endless tedium), then their participation in homosexual activity may be seen as mandatory not voluntary. Hence, this behavior cannot acquire *dispositional* status. In a harsher environment, the pressures to participate are greater, and the attribution to dispositions is diminished (Kelly, 1973). The exception are inmates who apparently (through manifestations like "feminine" gestures, or articulations) seem to endorse homosexuality and who presumably could have imported previously established sexual lifestyles into the prison.

How have these propositions been derived? There are foremost in the literature the more generic prison-environment studies which profile the inmates' world views and how they see themselves and others fitting into prison subcultures. These are typified by time-worn classics like Clemmer (1940) and Sykes (1958) and even some excellent popular novels (cf. *Falconer,* 1975, by John Cheever). Then there are numerous nomothetic accounts, primarily work from the 50s and 60s which used traditional sociological interview, observation, and survey techniques and usually relied on univariate analytic procedures. These comprise the bulk of evidence; they are nomothetic in the sense that they produced lengthy lists of names for roles inmates occupy. They describe the world of gorillas, punks, sissys, bulldykes, daggers, fems, jailhouse turnouts, and more. The labels are accompanied by explanations about the role and about why some inmates gravitate toward or are forced into these roles. Females are largely neglected in the assemblage probably because there are fewer female inmates and they are less violent, not because they are less active sexually.[4] The literature is built upon studies using inmate testimony and in several cases, there are historic accounts by authors who were convicted felons serving time in prison.

Three exceptions to the generic and nomothetic approaches are studies by Davis (1968), Lockwood (1980) and the Federal study. Davis' study is different from mainstream sociology because it is largely atheoretical. It is a documentary about the extent of exploitation in a system that was out of control in the late 60s.[5] Lockwood's excellent study appeared about the same time as the Federal study. Lockwood used several sampling strategies, studied several prisons, and used solid interview techniques. The study is limited to the New York State system unfortunately, but it did produce a fine and sensitive treatment of the topic. Another departure, more social psy-

---

[4]Noteworthy exceptions being works by Propper (1981), Ward and Kassenbaum (1965) and Giallombardo (1966).

[5]Davis and his associates interviewed virtually every inmate in the Philadelphia system to determine the extent of victimization in prisons, jails, and the vans used to transport inmates to and from court. He found 156 assaults on 97 victims by 176 aggressors. Since the sample represented about 5% of the inmates who were processed through the system during the study period, Davis estimated that perhaps as many as 2,000 assaults on 1,500 victims could have occurred during the 26 month period he investigated.

chological than sociological, the Federal study relies on multivariate analytic procedures, permitting the development and testing of complicated models of inmate behavior, and it sampled from the entire Federal prison system, permitting the establishment of baseline statistics as a yardstick for future investigations.

THE FEDERAL STUDY

Method, Procedures, Instruments

Readers should refer to the full report for a complete description of the study's methods and procedures (Nacci and Kane, 1984). Briefly, the study used a survey approach. Subjects were 330 inmate volunteers selected randomly from a proportional (stratified) sample of 17 Federal prisons. The interviewer was a male black ex-offender who traveled across the country to conduct all of the interviews. Subjects were males. Subject representativeness of the Bureau of Prisons male inmate population was confirmed in several analyses. Interviews were private and strictly confidential. In each of the 17 institutions a self-administering survey was distributed to the correctional officer complement.

The inmate survey was constructed to: (1) discover the extent of inmate victimization, and the amount of inmate homosexual activity; (2) provide information about the etiology of these behaviors; and, (3) suggest procedures to control inmate aggression based on information produced in the survey.[6]

Theoretical Assumption

A central assumption of the project concerns the matter of controlling homosexual activity because its existence is problematic. Later in the paper, there is a discussion about proposition 5 and why the Federal Bureau of Prisons endorses the control position. The goal of the Federal project all along has been to increase understanding, and consequently to make prisons safer through greater control of homosexual activity. The authors agreed early in the study that

---

[6]The correctional officer survey was developed to determine how aware officers are about matters related to inmate sex and aggression and what they believe is their responsibility to control these behaviors.

the methods, procedures, and instruments would be generic, and geared expressly toward increasing our understanding of inmate sexual and aggressive behaviors; the matter of development of procedures "to control" would therefore follow naturally from enhanced understanding.

FINDINGS

Findings from the Federal project have confirmed or disconfirmed both theoretical propositions from prior research and original conceptualizations from the Federal study. Some of those contributions are abstracted here, including racial bases of sexual assault, management problems involving assault victims and participants in homosexual activity, and administrative adjustments that reduce the threat of sexual violence and sex-related assaults.

Race and Sexual Assault

Racial conflict has been accorded casual status in the explanation of sexual assault in prison (Scacco, 1975). However, data obtained in the Federal study strongly challenge the racial conflict postulate, suggesting equally plausible interpretations involving target characteristics and racial differences in the use of coercive power. The Federal project confirmed sexual assault patterns found in previous research (Davis, 1968; Lockwood, 1980) that involved a predominance of white targets, black assailants, and black aggressor-white victim cases. From such findings one might infer that sexual assaults are a form of coercion selected by blacks to assert domination over whites in interracial conflict. However, using assault events as the unit of racial analysis, the Federal data revealed that black and white assailants victimized white targets at similar rates, 82% and 88% respectively. Hence, from the perspective of assailants, differences in black versus white target characteristics—like physical appearance or the likelihood of retaliation—may explain the predominant selection of white victims by both black and white assailants. The prevalence of black assailants is accounted for by the fact that blacks were more likely to be involved in gang rapes. This pattern, confirmed in the Davis, Lockwood, and Federal projects, warrants the inference that black and white aggressors employ different strategies of coercive power: that is, in potentially volatile situations blacks are more likely to coalesce, mounting strength in numbers.

Another source of information is tapped in the Federal study that disconfirms the racial conflict interpretation of sexual assaults. Inmate interviewees were asked to specify the primary reasons why sexual assaults occur in prison. Less than 1% offered race as a causal interpretation.

Attitudes Toward Homosexuality

Profiles obtained in the Federal study revealed that both targets of sexual assault and participants in consensual homosexual activity have attitudes that are favorable toward homosexuality as an orientation, affiliate with other prisoners involved in various forms of homosexual behavior, and more importantly, discuss sex often with other inmates. Hence, any public act endorsing homosexuality may contribute to being selected as a target.

Through effective staff training, line employees can be made aware of the cues attended to by assailants in selecting victims. In turn, correctional procedures and management practices that nurture good staff-inmate relations, wherein employees communicate to inmates the dangers of endorsement, whether attitudinal or behavioral, also contribute to a safer prison environment.

Volatility: Target Plus Assailant

The Federal study revealed that, in contrast with the general population, the typical target is tall, slender, wears his hair long, and appears effeminate; as a child experienced much social disorganization—broken marriage, unhappy parent-child relationships, parents with heavy drinking problems; is criminally sophisticated, with values, attitudes and predispositions shaped in America's institutions; is passive in interpersonal conflicts, except in sex related conflicts where he accepts that violent solutions are necessary. The Federal findings on the target's physical stature, non-violent disposition, and prior institutionalization confirm secondary data from other research.

Assaulters, on the other hand, are average in weight, but are larger than their target; they are younger than the average inmate, but older than their victim; they have a history of violence, are likely to have been committed for a violent crime, and are likely to be among the small group of inmates who frequently break prison rules. Typically, assaulters come from large urban areas, have had many juvenile commitments, but have received an average amount of education before incarceration; they are normal in mental stability and show no unusual tendencies toward self-destruction (cf. Moss and Hosford, 1979).

By virtue of the interaction of target and assailant characteristics, the target is singled out by assailants quickly as one who (1) is generally weak and exploitable and (2) "appropriately" feminine. This volatile combination of circumstances, coupled with the fact that the environment is geographically restricted and avoidance is difficult makes the case of sex pressuring mortally dangerous.

Normalization: Making Societal Norms Salient in Prison

In response to prior evidence that homosexual activity leads to violence, the Federal project pursued further knowledge of factors that encourage or discourage consensual participation. Traditional management techniques used to deter individual inmates from participating include separation, a cell assignment in less public housing, and counseling; of course, these methods require detection and reporting by staff.

Common sense suggests that normalization should occur through inmates' involvement in prison programs like furloughs or visits and that this should encourage abstinence from homosexual activity. However, the Federal findings do not show a relationship between involvement in furloughs or visits and abstinence from sex-related activities.

A social psychological model of normalization was adopted in the Federal study which assumes that the prediction of behavior is significantly facilitated by knowledge of the individual's attitudes toward the behavior in question and relevant behavioral norms endorsed by the person's significant others (Ajzen and Fishbein, 1972). Attitudes are continually changing; individuals accommodate new information by incorporating it into their belief matrices. Attitudes influence behavior; and norms—others' conventions for social behavior with sanctions prescribed for violations—influence both attitudes and behavior. From this model, it was predicted that inmates' abstinence from homosexual activity is strengthened by attitudes that do not favor homosexuality, but that do include a commitment to traditional religious beliefs; and that these attitudes and abstinence will be strengthened by the salience of endorsements made by the inmate's family, prison peers, and prison staff for norms that proscribe involvement in homosexual activity. The predictions were confirmed in the Federal findings. Clearly, the importance of the role embodied by institution staff as agents of normalization is documented. Line staff are in a position to influence inmates' attitudes about the appropriateness of behavior both within and outside of prison. Furthermore, by reinforcing societal norms and administrative proscriptions that discourage participation, line staff preclude the by-products of participation including sex-related aggression and a potential dilemma of self-concept for participants whose sexual identities are heterosexual.

The Incidence of Sexual Aggression

Results of the Federal study document that sexual aggression is uncommon in the Federal prison system. Data were obtained both from inmate interviews and the "archive" of recorded assaults.

Self Reports

Extrapolating from interview self-report data, the likelihood that an inmate would be forced to perform undesired sexual acts in a Federal institution is 6 in 1,000; and the chances that a prisoner would be sodomized are 3 in 1,000. Furthermore, interviews with inmates who have spent similar amounts of time incarcerated in Federal and non-Federal prisons indicated that assault rates are lower in Federal facilities. The difference may be due to differences in populations, treatment programs, or inmate management procedures. The Federal system employs a risk-assessment classification system that effectively assigns inmates to required levels of institution security and staff supervision (Kane and Saylor, 1983). A standardized intrainstitution management system (Levinson and Gerard, 1973) establishes the frequency and type of staff-inmate interaction that yields effective surveillance, nurtures the normalization influence of staff on inmates and, consequently, should inhibit sexual assault and sex-related aggression. Furthermore, each Federal institution offers a variety of programs from education and vocational training to counseling or work in prison industries. Certainly, involvement in such programs reduces idle time that could otherwise be spent by inmates in less structured situations having a greater prepotency of conflict and aggression. In fact, recent research (Petersilia, Honig, and Hubay, 1980) has substantiated an inverse relationship between participation in prison programs and involvement in institution misconduct.

The Archive

The Federal project studied sexual aggression through analyses of officially recorded assaults in addition to interviews. Two archival studies have been completed: an analysis of sex-related assaults over a five year period from 1973 to 1977; and a recent one year update, from October 1982 through September 1983 that included both sex-related and non-sex-related assaults. Both time periods revealed a rate of "known" sexual assaults in the Federal prison system of approximately 2 per month. The recent one year study further showed that the proportion of total assaults comprised by sex-related aggression is 9.5%, a much lower rate than the 25% uncovered by Toch (1968) in state facilities. Again, differences in assault rates may be due to a variety of prison system differences involving inmate populations, treatment, or management practices.

Overall, both inmate interviews and archival analyses reveal that rates of sexual aggression are low in Federal institutions. The continual monitoring of recorded sexual assaults from archival sources is desirable. Assuming continuity in procedures for investigating and recording assaults, the ratio of recorded to unreported sexual assaults should be constant. Hence, if the recorded number begins to climb, additional research procedures like inmate and staff interviews and contextual analyses must be used to examine the prison system dynamics that account for the increase in sexual aggression.

PROPOSITION FIVE: THE CONTROL OF CONSENSUAL HOMOSEXUAL ACTIVITY— THE CONTROVERSY—THE EVIDENCE

Proposition five, "that consensual homosexual activity is dangerous, destructive, and leads to violence among prison inmates" is a central theme in the Federal research project. Furthermore, the research indicates that consensual homosexual activity is problematic and hence, that it should be sanctioned. There are other points of view.[7]

Freedom of Sexual Expression

There is a trend in the country to decriminalize homosexual behavior in free society (see Vetri, 1980, Rivera, 1982). In 1962 sexual behavior between persons of the same sex was illegal in all 50 states. In 1982 private consensual adult sexual behavior was legal in 21 states; at last count there were 27 states with consenting adult laws which include sodomy. In many states, therefore, homosexual activity in prisons can be sanctioned because it violates state law; but in most states, it does *not* violate state law. This is not to say that legality of a behavior in the free community would have a bearing on whether the behavior should be accepted in prison. No one would argue that heterosexual activity *ought* to be available to inmates because it is permissible in free society. Rather, the argument—that homosexual behavior is illegal and hence, should be banned in prison—is becoming less and less germane. Neither is homosexual behavior any longer considered an organic disease having been absent from the American Medical Association's list of psychiatric disorders for more than a decade. Therefore, in most states, disallowance of homosexual behavior in prison must be for reasons other than illegality in the general community, or that it is thought by persons in the medical community to be a bona fide illness. The authority of corrections officials to deny consensual homosexual behavior falls under the rubric of behaviors contrary to the orderly operation of the facility.[8]

Proponents of greater sexual freedom believe that sexual depriva-

---

[7]The proposition relates to consensual homosexual activity. Although few would argue that sexual assaults among prisoners should *not* be deterred, such arguments are not beyond thinking. An unsettling "application" of sexual aggression would be threats made against inmates by administrators that they might be locked up with an aggressive homosexual inmate, and raped unless there is some desired change in behavior or "attitude." There is no evidence that this occurs in Federal prisons and it seems likely that it seldom occurs in most prisons and jails. It is hard to believe that any administrator could support this position—it is totally contrary to the movement toward greater personal liability of corrections officials who act without regard to acceptable correctional standards or who ignore inmate constitutional guarantees (see Cohn, 1983 for an excellent review of recent court rulings on personal liability related to inmate sexual aggression). Also see American Correctional Association's standards for correctional facilities and jails.

[8]In court cases litigants rely on scientific, anecdotal, and experimental evidence; the matter reduces to whether the court accepts the administration's contention that homosexual activity causes administrative problems and/or makes prisons less safe. In a relevant class action suit, *(Abbott v. Richardson)* plantiffs argued that magazines containing explicit erotic

tion constitutes cruel and unusual punishment, and hence, conflicts with constitutional guarantees, and that a policy of control unnecessarily restricts individual liberty. The issue will be resolved in court cases which evaluate constitutionality of prison conditions. In one important case, related to the crowding issue, the ruling suggests that public attitude about what constitutes cruel and unusual punishment plays an increasingly important role. In a footnote to the opinion in *Chapman v. Rhodes* issued by Justice Powell (425, U.S. 337, 1981) the court held that, "indeed, generalized opinions cannot weigh as heavily in determining contemporary standards of decency as, 'the public attitude toward a given sanction' " (a reference to *Gregg v. Georgia*, 428, U.S., 153, 173).

The concept of cruel and unusual punishment changes over time; what was legal treatment of offenders in 1920 may constitute unnecessarily harsh treatment in 1984. The trend toward decriminalization of homosexual activity reflects a more aggressive posture by groups representing gay rights; it may or may not reflect the liberalization of American opinions about homosexual activity (cf. Knutson).[9] For corrections administrators, a salient counter-pressure toward stricter treatment for criminals is immediate and contradicts the proposal for sexual freedom.

THE CONTROL POSITION

The argument favoring restricted homosexual activity among prisoners is: (1) based on principles of equal treatment for inmates regardless of their sexual preference; (2) congruent with a philosophy of stricter treatment for prisoners; and (3) a conviction that there is a relationship between consensual homosexual activity in prison and prisoner violence.

Cruel and Unusual Punishment; Unnecessarily Harsh Treatment?

Prisons would be more pleasant for inmates if inmates (whatever their sexual preference) could engage in sexual activity with their preferred sex partners. Whether disallowance of the privilege to do

---

depictions should be generally available in Federal prisons. The Government argued that literature could be inciteful or a cue that inmates would use it to find sex partners for either consensual or forced homosexual activities. A central theme, therefore, is the Government's belief that homosexual activity should be deterred because it conflicts with their mandate to keep prisoners free from harm.

[9]Public attitudes are not unaffected by court victories; prejudice against homosexuals could be, in part *because* the behavior was (is) illegal.

this constitutes unnecessarily harsh treatment is a matter for the courts to consider.[10]

From the corrections officials' perspective deterrence of homosexual activity is *not* unnecessarily harsh treatment. They understand that if they permit homosexual inmates to participate freely in sex, that would constitute an inequity for heterosexual inmates, and that they would soon be pressured to operate "family visitation" programs for all inmates. Administrators are generally disinterested in operating family visit programs. Most would probably agree that the danger associated with consensual homosexual activity is minimal in some types of prisons (e.g., camps, co-correctional facilities, or other places in the minimum to low medium security range), and therefore that they *could* permit greater sexual freedom there without endangering inmates.

There are six states that we are aware of operating family visitation programs where inmates can sign into a special area in the prison, trailers usually, and be with spouses and family for an extended, private visit. Administrative review of these programs is mixed, however, some administrators seem pleased. Family visitation programs operate across the full range of prison security levels. The risk of operating a family visitation program is directly related to the security level of the facility. In more secure settings, administrators are necessarily concerned about the introduction of contraband (drugs, weapons) and escapes—both are made easier by close-quarters visitation programs.

The benefits associated with programs, in terms of greater family stability, keeping families intact, and normalization, are relatively constant across security levels and a very desirable program derivative. But in practical terms, from the corrections officials' perspective, there is not much to gain from operating the program in medium or minimum security settings. For example, in the Federal Prison System, approximately one-third of inmates are in lower security, more open prison settings. Many inmates there qualify and receive overnight furloughs partly because the danger associated with the introduction of contraband is negligible. Because furlough programs are relatively inexpensive while family visit programs are

---

[10]Sexual behavior does not serve a fundamental life sustaining "need" and is primarily only in the sense that it is necessary for species (not individual) survival. When deciding whether denial of access to a consenting sex partner is or is not unnecessarily harsh, also consider that sexual relief is available through masturbation, nocturnal emission, and fantasy.

more difficult and expensive to formulate and to run, officials favor the former over the latter.

In the higher security prisons and penitentiaries, the benefits to administrators *could* be great depending on how the program was structured. Certainly the danger associated with introduction of contraband and the pressure to keep inmates from escaping are greater. But a family visit program would be a unique and powerful form of social control for administrators—participation would be highly desired by inmates and the threat of removal of that privilege would be helpful for keeping prisoners in line. To pay dividends for administrators, in these pragmatic social control terms, the program would have to be available for more disruptive prisoners as well as for the general population. These are that minority of inmates referred to earlier—the three percent of the inmate population who account for about 90% of institution violence. Unfortunately, these inmates have lengthy criminal careers spanning decades and have generally disrupted family lives as well. Would they have spouses? Would administrators endorse "convenience" marriages so there could be a family visit? Would prostitutes be permitted to visit inmates in American prisons as they now do in some European and Latin American jails and prisons? Would homosexual inmates be permitted to spend a family visit with "spouses"—with lovers?

Stricter Treatment for Prisoners

Greater control of sexual activity in prison is congruent with current correctional ideology. The current Comprehensive Crime Control Bill (currently before the House and passed by the Senate) contains provisions for stricter, and surer fixed sentencing, with sentencing guidelines. This Bill signals a change in correctional ideology—away from indeterminism in sentencing, and toward a model of more strict and sure justice for criminals. Legislative actions and their administrative changes reveal that politicians and lawmakers believe that Americans favor a "get tough attitude with criminals." Sexual deprivation has always been an accepted condition of confinement. It is not surprising that administrators are reluctant to undertake programs like family visits—especially for inmates in penitentiaries (who presumably "deserve" greater punishment). The Supreme Court ruling in *Chapman v. Rhodes* has set the stage for corrections officials to be more, not less, attuned to public attitudes.

The Sex/Violence Connection

The empirical evidence to date indicates that homosexual activity and violence are associated, however, there is not unanimity among corrections officials on this issue.[11] There has never been a "poll" to determine the percentage of administrators who observed that their prisons, units, or wards were any freer from violence when homosexual activity was high. Resolution of the issue will rest in the hands of those who study prison archives.

Some proportion of the universe of violence in prisons is attributable to sexual activity and some proportion of sex-related aggression is manifested as sexual assaults. The parameters of these proportions were established by a special task force that studied violence in the California prison system (see Toch, 1965). One fourth of the aggression in that system was motivated by sexual activity, and that 25% was divided equivalently between pressure-related and consensual activity. An investigation conducted for the Federal Prison System by Henderson (1976) shows vividly how the consequences of consensual homosexual activity can be deadly; five of eight consecutive homicides in a Federal penitentiary were motivated by consensual homosexual activity. Nacci (1977) analyzed the major assaults referred to the F.B.I. for investigation during the same time period covered by the Henderson analysis; 25% of the cases were motivated by homosexual activity. Sylvester, Reed, and Nelson (1977) analyzed circumstances surrounding prison homicides occurring in calendar year 1973 in American prisons. There were 128 homicides in 54 of 170 prisons that house male felons with populations of 200 or more inmates. The record revealed that homosexual activity was the single most important motive for the murders; 27% of the homicides that were studied involved homosexuality as the primary or secondary motive.

EVOLVING PROCESSES THAT WILL REDUCE SEX-RELATED VIOLENCE

Some important evolving correctional "processes" will directly effect prison safety: all inmates will benefit. The first is the new role for the Federal Government. The role has changed dramatically

---

[11]In one speaking engagement administrators from a jail setting argued that their jails had been especially free from violence recently because the number of active homosexual inmates had increased. The administrators acknowledged that occasionally one took on more than he could handle and had to request segregation from other inmates for his own safety. In our

since the Carter Administration dismembered LEAA in the late 1970s. Previously, a primary role for the Government was to oversee and administer block grants to law enforcement agencies in state and local government; currently, the Government is exemplar, teacher, and partner to the states. The processes below are, in part, a consequence of this important change in role for the Government.

Better Risk Assessment Techniques

Inmates are assigned to prisons and to living quarters within prisons according to administration's assessment that the inmates are a "risk" to each other, to staff, and to the community (if they escape). Previously (and in many states today) risk assessment has been a subjective and somewhat arbitrary procedure. Objective risk assessment model programs were developed by the National Institute of Corrections and these are being transported to many state systems. Objective risk assessment techniques for classifying inmates in jails are being developed and validated by the Federal Bureau of Prisons. The importance of this, is that administrators will be able to identify and sort out weaker (less risky) inmates from more dangerous inmates.

Accreditation

In 1977, the Commission for Accreditation in Corrections promulgated *Volume 1 of Standards for Adult Correctional Institutions.* This began a national movement toward adult and juvenile prison and jail certification. The accreditation movement is especially effective in bringing states and government into alignment with accepted correctional standards; currently 351 American Federal and State prisons, jails, and programs have been accredited; 44 Canadian facilities and programs are accredited as well.

Training, Consultation, Information Sharing

In 1974, the National Institute of Corrections was established: to provide technical assistance and training to the states; to operate a National Information Clearinghouse; and to conduct a jail training

---

schema, aggression against a homosexual to perform sex against his will constitutes a sexual assault. Given the trend in court cases (where courts hold correctional officials *personally* liable for negligence) officials who look the other way or otherwise encourage homosexual activity are making a mistake that may cost them money as well as endangering inmates.

program at its center in Boulder, Colorado. A recent addition, the National Academy of Corrections, provides training for state and local authorities. The facility has been successful in providing much needed information about technical innovations and practical procedures.

Improvements in Architecture; Improved Surveillance Through Design Enhancements

The most dangerous prisons and jails are ones that are most difficult for staff to supervise. Large, open bay dormitories facilitate inmate violence and physical illness (cf. Gaes, 1984). Current building philosophy in jails and in prisons (endorsed by the American Correctional Association and promulgated in *Standards* by the Commission on Accreditation) establish minimum levels of personal space in living quarters, and specify individual cells for newly constructed or modified facilities. The Jail Center of the National Institute of Corrections assists states in adopting modern jail designs (exemplified by the Contra Costa, California model and the Metropolitan Community Center designs developed for the Bureau of Prisons).

The importance of these trends for *all* inmates needs to be emphasized. With regard to greater safety, *specifically* for victims or targets of sexual assault, it should be emphasized that sexual aggression is a form of more generic "aggression," and as such its occurrence should be proportional to overall level of institution violence. Sexual aggression is "different" in one important respect—staff can become inured about protecting inmates. Victimization invites attributions from staff that the victim got what he deserved because he was "homosexual" or was interested in sex in the first place. The Federal Prison System has adopted a strategy designed to increase awareness among staff about the environmental pressures on inmates to participate, that victims are usually heterosexuals and that homosexuals are likely targets for assaults. The strategy is built on a fundamental belief that better understanding—through training—will ultimately make officers more diligent about supervising heterosexual, bisexual, and homosexual inmates. A training module on inmate sexual aggression is being prepared for the National Academy of Corrections and will be available soon—many ideas from the Federal study will be incorporated.

Exposing these matters of sexual aggression reveals flaws in investigation and procedures for gathering evidence. It is imperative that assaulters be identified, adjudicated, and sanctioned. The process relies on timely and accurate evidentiary gathering procedures. Most police departments use pre-packaged "rape kits" (administered by physicians) for gathering and preserving rape-related evidence; successful prosecution of rapists is difficult otherwise. We doubt that most prison and jail systems use these techniques and encourage them to do so.

BIBLIOGRAPHY

Abbott v. Richardson, U.S. District Court for D. C. 1047-73.
Ajzen, I. and Fishbein, M. Attitudes and normative beliefs as factors influencing behavioral intentions. *Journal of Personality and Social Psychology,* 1972, *21,* 1-9.
American Correctional Association Standards for Correctional Facilities. Available from the A.C.A., College Park, MD. 20740.
Bartollas, C., Miller, S.J. and Dinitz, S. *Juvenile victimization.* New York: Sage Publication, 1976.
Brownmiller, S. *Against our will.* New York: Simon & Schuster, 1975.
Carter, R.M., Glaser, D., and Wilkens, L.T. (eds.) *Correctional institutions, Third Edition,* New York: Harper and Row, 1984.
Chapman v. Rhodes, 425, U.S. 337 (1981).
Cheever, J. *Falconer.* New York: Ballantine Books, 1975.
Clemmer, D. *Some aspects of sexual behavior in the prison community.* Proceedings of the Eighty-eighth Annual Congress of the American Correctional Association, Detroit, Michigan, 1958, 377-385.
Cohn, D.B. *Institutional violence and sexual assault.* Unpublished manuscript presented at the City of New York, Department of Corrections "Workshop on Sexual Aggression," New York, New York, December, 1983.
Davis, A. J. Sexual assaults in the Philadelphia Prison System and sheriff's vans. *Transaction,* 1968, 8-16.
Dollard, J., Doob, L., Miller, N., Mowrer, O. and Sears, R. *Frustration and aggression,* New Haven: Yale University Press, 1939.
Gaes, G.G. *The courts, corrections, and crowding: A critical review of prison crowding research and its relation to legal, legislative, and correctional communities.* Federal Bureau of Prisons Office of Research Report, January, 1984, *R-2,* NER-1
Giallombardo, R. *Society of women: A study of woman's prisons.* New York: John Wiley & Sons, Inc., 1966.
Kane, T.R. and Saylor, W.G. *Security designation and custody classification of inmates.* Research report U.S. Bureau of Prisons. Washington, D. C.
Kelley, H.H. The process of causal attribution. *American Psychologist.* 1973, *28,* 107-128.
Levinson, R. and Gerard, R. Functional units: a differential correctional approach. *Federal Probation,* December, 1973, 8-16.
Lockwood, D. *Prison sexual violence.* New York: Elsevier North Holland, 1980.
Moss, C.S., Hosford, R.E. and Anderson, W.R. Sexual assault in prison. *Psychological Reports,* 1979, *44,* 823-828.
Nacci, P.L. *Homosexuality at the U.S. Penitentiary, Lewisburg.* Unpublished manuscript U.S. Federal Prison System, Office of Research, Washington, D.C., 1976.
Nacci, P.L. and Kane, T.R. Sex and sexual aggression in Federal prisons. In *Progress Reports,* Robert Levinson (Ed.), Federal Bureau of Prisons, Washington, D.C. 20534, 1982.

Nacci, P.L. and Kane, T.R. The incidence of sex and sexual aggression in Federal prisons. *Federal Probation,* December, 1983, 31-36.

Nacci, P.L. and Kane, T.R. Sex and sexual aggression in Federal prisons: Inmate involvement and employee impact. *Federal Probation,* April, 1984.

Nacci, P.L. and Kane, T.R. *Sex and sexual aggression in prison.* New York: The Haworth Press, in Press, 1984.

Petersilia, J., Honig, P. and Hubay, P., Jr. *The prison experience of career criminals.* Report published by The Rand Corporation, Santa Monica, CA. 90406.

Propper, A.M. *Prison homosexuality.* Toronto: Lexington Books, 1981.

Scacco, A.M. *Rape in prison.* Springfield, Illinois: Thomas, 1975.

Shore, D.A. *Sex related issues in correctional facilities; a classified bibliography.* Chicago: Playboy Foundation, 1981.

Sykes, G.M. *The Society of captives.* Princeton, N.J.: Princeton University Press, 1958.

Sylvester, S.F., Reed, J.H. and Nelson, D.O. *Prison homicides.* New York: Spectrum Publications, 1977.

Toch, H. Normatively hostile, purposefully hostile, or disinhibited bloody angry? *Journal of Research in Crime and Delinquency,* 1978, *15*(2), 162-165.

Ward, D.A. and Kassenbaum, G.G. *Women's prison: Sex and social structure.* Chicago: Aldine, 1965.

Wolfgang, M.E. and Ferricuti, F. *The subculture of violence toward an integrated theory in criminology.* New York: Tavistock Publications, 1967.

Wooden, W.S. and Parker, J. *Men behind bars; sexual exploitation in prison.* New York: Plenum Press, 1982.

Gender Disparity
in the Setting of Bail:
Prostitution Offenses in Buffalo, NY
1977-1979

Frances P. Bernat

INTRODUCTION

Pretrial release has been the subject of much debate in the United States for over twenty years. A portion of this debate has focused upon whether the bail system has treated accused persons without funds for bail differently than those with funds for bail. During the 1960s, critics of the bail system began to press for reforms which would allow for a greater number of persons to be released pending the disposition of their criminal charges, regardless of their ability to post bail. Forrest Dill, in his examination of bail bondsmen, in 1975, observed:

> Numerous attempts to reform the bail system have been launched over the last fifteen years. Perhaps surprisingly, appellate courts have had no direct influence on this development. As Caleb Foote observed ten years ago, bail reform has been "the only major reform of recent decades in which the courts have played a wholly passive role."[1]

Bail reforms occurred in many states through legislative changes of bail code provisions. In New York State, much of the reform in pretrial release statutes became effective in 1971.[2] The New York bail reforms were designed to bring a "fresh structural and phraseological approach" to the subject of bail by redrafting or

---

Frances P. Bernat is Assistant Professor in Criminal Justice, Department of Political Science, Washington State University.

21

eliminating "the most archaic and poorly drafted" provisions on bail that then existed.[3]

While New York has never recognized an absolute right to bail,[4] the state does provide for a statutory right to bail in non-felony cases and for a discretionary right to bail in felony cases.[5] Because this paper analyzes a substantive criminal law offense which is not a felony,[6] only the criminal procedure law provisions on bail which apply in the non-felony situation will be discussed.

The statutory right to bail, in a non-felony situation, may be effectuated by police when the accused is arrested;[7] and/or by the court when the accused is arraigned.[8] Initially, the police have the option to detain or release an accused at the stationhouse. A decision by the police to allow an accused to be released may engender one of two possible results: the police may decide to release an individual outright, on his or her own recognizance,[9] or, place the burden of release on the accused by requiring that the accused post pre-arraignment bail.[10] Thus, the New York legislature permits the police to act in the place of the arraignment judge, at an earlier stage in the judicial process, for the purposes of making pretrial release decisions. A judge, at the accused's arraignment, faces decisions similar to those faced by the police. Although a judge must not refuse to set bail, the judge has to decide whether to release an accused on his or her own recognizance, or, to require bail and place the burden of release on the accused.

In New York, the only legitimate purpose for setting bail is to ensure an accused's (continued) presence in court;[12] the amount of bail that may be set must not exceed an amount which would be necessary for such a purpose.[13] The state legislature revised the bail procedures in partial recognition of past inequities in the system. The revision provides for pretrial via bail forms which are, or may be, the least burdensome for an accused; for example, an accused may be released on bail via an unsecured bail bond, or a partially secured bail bond.[14]

The intended effect of the state's bail code revisions is to release a greater number of persons who are awaiting trial, regardless of socioeconomic status. Because misdemeanors are non-serious offenses, additional justifications have been offered for the allowance of pre-arraignment bail, or release on one's own recognizance at the stationhouse. These justifications include: saving police resources and providing a less "inconvenient" and "jarring clash with the state and the police" on the part of the accused.[15]

This paper aims to determine whether the actual effects of New York's bail reform reflect the intended effects of the reform measures. Because the police may make bail decisions in lieu of an arraignment judge, decisions made by both the police and arraignment judge will be analyzed. John R. Baumann has analyzed bail reform in the United States. He argues that the bail reform measures instituted since the 1960s are "saving those already saved and forsaking those who have always been forsaken."[16] Specifically, Baumann claims:

> The explanation for this lack of substantive change is not to be found in either deficiencies of implementation nor evil intentions. Rather, we need to look back at the factors which determine eligibility and recognize the blatant class character of each of them. With this in mind, we should not be at all surprised at the ineffectiveness of bail reform legislation. Bail reform has not, however, been totally "unsuccessful"; but its accomplishments have tended to be tangential to the real issues and problems of bail. . . . Bail reform gives the facade of meaningful reform while basically altering nothing in a meaningful fashion. . . . Bail reform thus managed to deflect the challenges being laid before the judiciary, giving the impression of dynamic and progressive change and yet preserving in its most important details a system of justice based on discrimination and class oppression for working-class defendants.[17]

Baumann's assertions strike a blow at bail reform legislation because, if he is correct, then bail reform has been an ineffective tool in combating the problems of discrimination the intended reforms were designed to attack.

Goldkamp and Gottfredson studied factors which influence bail decisions. They divided the bail decision-making process into three steps: a decision to release an accused on his or her own recognizance; a decision to release an accused on bail; and, the specific amount of bail to impose or require.[18] In regard to the first step, they found that the variable which explained the most variance (29%) was the present charge against the accused.[19] In addition, variables which Goldkamp and Gottfredson termed demographic (age, race, sex, employment history, wages), health (narcotics use, hospitalization, etc.) and, legal (suretys, counsel, etc.) did not explain much variance and, therefore, were not determined to influence bail decisions.[20] Because the analysis at the first step had already screened the accused, a judge's knowledge that the accused had used weapons when committing crimes was a main factor in later cash bail decisions.[21]

This paper will focus on the bail decision-making process as it is applied when an accused has been arrested for a prostitution offense. In particular, pretrial released decisions will be examined in order to determine whether gender-based classifications exist. A pretrial release decision may not be based on gender. Such a classification may violate equal protection principles and will be given "scrutiny" by an appellate court upon review.[22] By focusing on the relationship between gender and pretrial release with one particular offense, it is hoped that a better understanding of the complex factors involved in pretrial release decisions may be reached.

METHODOLOGY

The source of the data used in this study is the Buffalo, New York, Criminal Court records. Data was collected from court files which indicated that a defendant was arrested for prostitution activity[23] between January 1, 1977 and December 31, 1979. A total of 809 cases was utilized, representing every filed case which was closed by the time that data collection was begun.[24]

The main issue addressed in this study is what types of people were released at what points during the bail-setting procedure. In this regard, the dependent variable is whether pretrial release occurred, and if so, at what point of time. The dependent variable will be referred to as a defendant's pretrial release status.

Pretrial release, as indicated above, may occur at two points of time; after arrest, and/or after arraignment. Thus, the dependent variable has six potential categories. These categories are: (1) released on bail; (2) released on one's own recognizance; (3) never released; (4) released by the police, but subsequently detained after arraignment; (5) detained, but subsequently released on one's own recognizance; and, (6) detained, but subsequently released on bail.

The distribution of these six categories is shown in Table 1. It is shown that: 8.8 percent of the accused were *released on bail* by both the police and the court; 7.7 percent were *released* by both the police and the court on their *own recognizance;* 20.5 percent were

TABLE 1

Description of an accused's pretrial release status

(809 = 100.0%)

	No.	%
Accused released both at the stationhouse and after arraignment on bail	71	8.8
Accused released both at the stationhouse and after arraignment on their own recognizance	62	7.7
Accused never released	166	20.5
Accused released at the stationhouse on own recognizance or bail, but detained after arraignment for failure to post bail set by judge	5	0.6
Accused detained at the stationhouse, but released after arraignment on their own recognizance	174	21.5
Accused detained at the stationhouse, but released after posting bail set by the judge	213	26.3
Cases missing information	118	14.6
Total	809	100.0

never released before trial; 0.6 percent were *released* by police, *but subsequently detained* after their arraignment due to a failure to post bail set by a judge; 21.5 percent were initally *detained* by the police, *but were released on their own recognizance* by a judge; and finally, 26.3 percent were initially *detained* by the police, *but were released on bail* which was set by a judge. These six categories will be collapsed in order that further statistical analysis would not be hampered by the occurrence of small figures in crosstabulation cells. The new dependent variable categories are: Release; Detention; Release-Detention; and, Detention-Release. The Release category means that an accused was neither detained at the stationhouse nor after arraignment because either the accused posted bail, or, no bail was required to be posted. The Detention category means that an accused was neither released at the stationhouse nor after arraignment. The Release-Detention category means that an accused was released at the stationhouse on pre-arraignment bail or on recognizance, but was subsequently detained after arraignment for failure to post bail. This category will be deleted from this study due to the small number of cases involved (N = 5). Finally, the Detention-Release category means that release was not obtained at the stationhouse, but was had after arraignment because the accused posted bail or was released on his or her own recognizance.

Because the only valid purpose of bail in New York is to assure the presence of the defendent in court, it is necessary to assess the effect of certain variables on the likelihood of a defendant's failure to reappear in court. Two recent studies will be discussed. Clarke, Freeman and Koch found in their study of bail risks that the factor which most affected a defendant's reappearance rate was the court's disposition time; the longer the court took to reach a final disposition the greater the likelihood the defendant would not reappear.[25] Factors which did not affect a defendant's likelihood of reappearance were sex, race, income, employment status, or the offense charged (although the authors were not as certain as to their conclusion concerning the offense-charged variable).[26] Similar results were reached in a study conducted by the Cleveland State Law Review. The study found that if a defendant was closely supervised while released from custody, the accused was most likely to reappear. Variables which were found not to affect reappearance rates were the type of bail, amount of bond, and community ties.[27] Thus, regardless of age, race, sex or criminal history, bail risks were found to be most closely associated with the ability to maintain contact with the defendant's.[28]

Although gender was not found to be a valid indicator of one's bail risk, it is expected that more females, than males, will be detained before trial. Therefore, the sole independent variable is gender. The hypothesis of this study is that females arrested for prostitution will not be released from pretrial custody as often, or as quickly, as males. It is expected that females will not be released at the stationhouse and will be required to post bail more often than males before their release may be had. This expectation is based upon the belief that gender will be shown to be a factor which undermines New York's bail reform legislation. Other variables will be used as a control on the relationship between gender and pretrial release status in this study. These control variables are: offense charged; residence; age; race; type of defense attorney retained; judge; year of the offense; amount of bail; whether another offense was charged at the time of the arrest; employment status; and, form of bail. It is believed that some of these variables may affect the manner in which a judge views the probability that an accused will reappear in court (offense, race, age, residence, judge, employment status, and other offenses charged) even if they have not empirically been shown to be related to a defendant's bail risk. Other control variables may indicate the ability of an accused to post bail if required, and, thus, secure his or her own release (amount of bail, form of bail, and employment status).

RESULTS

The relationship of the dependent variable, pretrial release status, with the independent variable, gender, is presented in Table 2. The table shows the majority of women (63.2 percent) were not released until after their arrest, but were instead detained at the stationhouse and released after their arraignment. In contrast, males were able to secure pretrial release after their arrest 36.6 percent of the time, while about an equal percentage of males (37.2 percent) were detained and released after their arraignment. Overall, the percentage of women who were not released until after their arraignment is greater than the total percentage of persons in this category (56.2 percent). The percentage of men who were released after their arrest is greater than the total percentage of persons released at the stationhouse (19.3 percent). Thus, males appear to have had a greater likelihood of stationhouse release than females; but, both sexes, if not released earlier, had a good likelihood of securing release after arraignment.

In order to determine whether these initial findings are accurate,

TABLE 2

EFFECT OF SEX ON PRE-TRIAL STATUS
(% may not add up to 100.0 due to rounding)

Pre-trial Status
1. By: SEX

	Females		Males		Total	
	No.	%	No.	%	No.	%
Release	64	12.9	67	36.6	131	19.3
Detain	118	23.8	48	26.2	166	24.5
Detain-Release	313	63.2	68	37.2	381	56.2
Total	495		183		678	

Chi Square Significance = 0.0000
Cramer's V = 0.28549

the relationship between gender and pretrial release status will be examined after a control variable has been added to the relationship.

Offense

This study focused on two offenses: prostitution and patronizing a prostitute. Sixty-three and two-tenths of a percent of females and 56.3 percent of males arrested for prostitution were detained after their arrest, but were released after their arraignment. In contrast, 73.6 percent of males arrested for patronizing were released after their arrest. In addition, male prostitutes were more likely to be unsuccessful in securing pretrial release than female prostitutes or male patrons. Therefore, the initial relationship of gender to pretrial release status is better explained by controlling for offense charged because all males do not have an equal chance for stationhouse release; only patrons are most likely to be released at the stationhouse.

Residence

As a community ties variable, residence may indicate the stability of a person; that is, if the person lives out of the court's jurisdiction, the person may be less likely to return to the court. The data indicates that there is a difference in pretrial release status between males who reside outside of the city limits and all females. In particular, 78.6 percent of males who were released at the stationhouse resided in the city's suburbs; 41.4 percent of males who reside in Canada or elsewhere were released at the stationhouse. In contrast, only 12.7 percent of women who reside within the city limits, 23.1 percent of women who reside in the city's suburbs and, 13.13 percent of women who reside in Canada or elsewhere were released at the stationhouse.

Age

Regardless of the female's age, the majority of females were released after their arraignment. In contrast, while young males were more likely to be released after their arraignment, older males were more likely to be released after their arrest.

TABLE 2, continued

2. By: SEX CONTROLLING FOR OFFENSE

Prostitution

	Females		Males		Total	
	No.	%	No.	%	No.	%
Release	64	13.0	3	3.1	67	11.4
Detain	118	23.9	39	40.6	157	26.6
Detain-Release	312	63.2	54	56.3	366	62.0
Total	494		96		590	

Chi Square Significance = 0.0003
Cramer's V = 0.16427

Patronizing

	Females		Males		Total	
	No.	%	No.	%	No.	%
Release	0	0.0	64	73.6	64	73.6
Detain	0	0.0	9	10.3	9	10.3
Detain-Release	0	0.0	14	16.1	14	16.1
Total	0		87		87	

Chi Square Significance =
Cramer's V =

3. By: SEX CONTROLLING FOR RESIDENCE

Buffalo City

	Females		Males		Total	
	No.	%	No.	%	No.	%
Release	58	12.7	35	28.2	93	16.0
Detain	108	23.6	32	25.8	140	24.1
Detain-Release	291	63.7	57	46.0	348	59.9
Total	457		124		581	

Chi Square Significance = 0.0000
Cramer's V = 0.18554

Buffalo Suburb

	Females		Males		Total	
	No.	%	No.	%	No.	%
Release	3	23.1	22	78.6	25	61.0
Detain	0	0.0	4	14.3	4	9.8
Detain-Release	10	76.9	2	7.1	12	29.3
Total	13		28		41	

Chi Square Significance = 0.0000
Cramer's V = 0.71757

TABLE 2, continued

Canada and other

	Females		Males		Total	
	No.	%	No.	%	No.	%
Release	2	13.3	10	41.7	12	30.8
Detain	7	46.7	9	37.5	16	41.0
Detain-Release	6	40.0	5	20.8	11	28.2
Total	15		24		39	

Canada:
Chi Square Significance = 0.3012
Cramer's v = 0.63246

Other:
Chi Square Significance = 0.0468
Cramer's V = 0.43076

4. By: SEX CONTROLLING FOR AGE

15-19

	Females		Males		Total	
	No.	%	No.	%	No.	%
Release	16	9.6	1	2.6	17	8.3
Detain	39	23.4	17	44.7	56	27.3
Detain-Release	112	67.1	20	52.6	132	64.4
Total	167		38		205	

Chi Square Significance = 0.0184
Cramer's V = 0.19737

20-24

	Females		Males		Total	
	No.	%	No.	%	No.	%
Release	28	15.1	15	25.4	43	17.6
Detain	39	21.0	16	27.1	55	22.4
Detain-Release	119	64.0	28	47.5	147	60.0
Total	186		59		245	

Chi Square Significance = 0.0628
Cramer's V = 0.15033

25-34

	Females		Males		Total	
	No.	%	No.	%	No.	%
Release	16	13.8	26	50.0	42	25.0
Detain	34	29.3	11	21.2	45	26.8
Detain-Release	66	56.9	15	28.8	81	48.2
Total	116		52		168	

Chi Square Significance = 0.0000
Cramer's V = 0.39020

35 and above

	Females		Males		Total	
	No.	%	No.	%	No.	%
Release	3	20.0	22	73.3	25	55.6
Detain	2	13.3	3	10.0	5	11.1
Detain-Release	10	66.7	5	16.7	15	33.3
Total	15		30		45	

Chi Square Significance = 0.0017
Cramer's V = 0.53166

Race

The data show that 55.4 percent of white males were released after their arrest. In contrast, the majority of females, white or black, and black males were released after their arraignment. Of any category, black males were less likely to be successful in securing pretrial release.

Judge

Of the three dependent variable categories, two must be considered when analyzing whether a particular judge treats accused persons differently on account of sex. These categories are Detain-Release, and Detain. When the total percentage of persons who were successful in securing release is reviewed, it appears that almost every judge handled the availability of pretrial release in essentially the same manner; i.e., the accused was able to secure release after the arraignment. However, when the data is analyzed by gender, it appears that female defendants had the most difficult time securing pretrial release when one of the following judges presided: Trammell, Rammuno, Forma, and Sims. In particular, of those women who were detained at the time of their arraignment: about one-third (15/48) were unable to secure release from Judge Trammell; about one-half (20/41) did not secure release from Judge Ramunno; about one-third (10/33) were unable to secure release from Judge Forma; and, about one-third (9/31) were unsuccessful in securing release from Judge Sims. Likewise, males who came before Judges Trammell, Kubiniec, Forma, Sedita, and Sims and who were seeking pretrial release for the first time may also have had difficulty in securing their release. In particular, males who sought release from Judge Trammell had the most difficulty in securing their release as more males remained in jail than were released by that judge, while about one-half of the males who came before Judges Kubiniec (5/11), Forma (6/12), Sedita (5/13) and Sims (6/15) were unable to secure pretrial release.

TABLE 2, continued

5. By: SEX CONTROLLING FOR RACE

Black

	Females		Males		Total	
	No.	%	No.	%	No.	%
Release	39	10.3	14	16.1	53	11.4
Detain	89	23.6	33	37.9	122	26.3
Detain-Release	249	66.0	40	46.0	289	62.3
Total	377		87		464	

Chi Square Significance = 0.0023
Cramer's V = 0.16170

White

	Females		Males		Total	
	No.	%	No.	%	No.	%
Release	23	23.2	46	55.4	69	37.9
Detain	25	25.3	12	14.5	37	20.3
Detain-Release	51	51.5	25	30.1	76	41.8
Total	99		83		182	

Chi Square Significance = 0.0000
Cramer's V = 0.33047

6. By: SEX CONTROLLING FOR JUDGE (50 cases or more)

Roberts

	Females		Males		Total	
	No.	%	No.	%	No.	%
Release	8	22.2	14	66.7	22	38.6
Detain	7	19.4	2	9.5	9	15.8
Detain-Release	21	58.3	5	23.8	26	45.6
Total	36		21		57	

Chi Square Significance = 0.0039
Cramer's V = 0.44090

TABLE 2, continued

Trammell

	Females		Males		Total	
	No.	%	No.	%	No.	%
Release	11	18.6	8	33.3	19	22.9
Detain	15	25.4	11	45.8	26	31.3
Detain-Release	33	55.9	5	20.8	38	45.8
Total	59		24		83	

Chi Square Significance = 0.0145
Cramer's V = 0.31940

Kubiniec

	Females		Males		Total	
	No.	%	No.	%	No.	%
Release	6	11.8	1	8.3	7	11.1
Detain	12	23.5	5	41.7	17	27.0
Detain-Release	33	64.7	6	50.0	39	61.9
Total	51		12		63	

Chi Square Significance = 0.4434
Cramer's V = 0.16068

McCarthy

	Females		Males		Total	
	No.	%	No.	%	No.	%
Release	7	15.2	3	50.0	10	19.2
Detain	6	13.0	2	33.3	8	15.4
Detain-Release	33	71.7	1	16.7	34	65.4
Total	46		6		52	

Chi Square Significance = 0.0270
Cramer's V = 0.37266

Sedita

	Females		Males		Total	
	No.	%	No.	%	No.	%
Release	4	10.5	9	40.9	13	21.7
Detain	7	18.4	5	22.7	12	20.0
Detain-Release	27	71.1	8	36.4	35	58.3
Total	38		22		60	

Chi Square Significance = 0.0114
Cramer's V = 0.38600

TABLE 2, continued

Ramunno

	Females		Males		Total	
	No.	%	No.	%	No.	%
Release	5	10.9	6	35.3	11	17.5
Detain	20	43.5	3	17.6	23	36.5
Detain-Release	21	45.7	8	47.1	29	46.0
Total	46		17		63	

Chi Square Significance = 0.0385
Cramer's V = 0.32158

Parlato

	Females		Males		Total	
	No.	%	No.	%	No.	%
Release	2	5.0	7	43.8	9	16.1
Detain	6	15.0	2	12.5	8	14.3
Detain-Release	32	80.0	7	43.8	39	69.6
Total	40		16		56	

Chi Square Significance = 0.0016
Cramer's V = 0.47966

Forma

	Females		Males		Total	
	No.	%	No.	%	No.	%
Release	2	5.7	9	42.9	11	19.6
Detain	10	28.6	6	28.6	16	28.6
Detain-Release	23	65.7	6	28.6	29	51.8
Total	35		21		56	

Chi Square Significance = 0.0017
Cramer's V = 0.47650

Sims

	Females		Males		Total	
	No.	%	No.	%	No.	%
Release	0	0.0	6	28.6	6	11.5
Detain	9	29.0	6	28.6	15	28.8
Detain-Release	22	71.0	9	42.9	31	59.6
Total	31		21		52	

Chi Square Significance = 0.0052
Cramer's V = 0.44973

Year

Over the three years studied, the percentage of females detained and/or released at some point of time in the pretrial process did not change dramatically. On the other hand, the percentage of males detained and/or released did change dramatically. In particular, women were detained at the stationhouse and released after their arraignment the majority of the time in 1977, 1978 and, 1979. In contrast, men were released at the stationhouse much more frequently in 1977 than in 1978 and 1979; the percent of men who were released at the stationhouse in 1977 was 68.3; in 1978, this figure dropped to 40.0 percent; and, in 1979, the figure dropped to a low of 16.9 percent of the males being released at the stationhouse.

TABLE 2, continued

7. By: SEX CONTROLLING FOR YEAR

1977

	Females		Males		Total	
	No.	%	No.	%	No.	%
Release	24	22.2	28	68.3	52	34.9
Detain	20	18.5	7	17.1	27	18.1
Detain-Release	64	59.3	6	14.6	70	47.0
Total	108		41		149	

Chi Square Significance = 0.0000
Cramer's V = 0.45395

1978

	Females		Males		Total	
	No.	%	No.	%	No.	%
Release	17	10.6	26	40.0	43	19.0
Detain	47	29.2	15	23.1	62	27.4
Detain-Release	97	60.2	24	36.9	121	53.5
Total	161		65		226	

Chi Square Significance = 0.0000
Cramer's V = 0.34199

1979

	Females		Males		Total	
	No.	%	No.	%	No.	%
Release	23	10.2	13	16.9	36	11.9
Detain	51	22.6	26	33.8	77	25.4
Detain-Release	152	67.3	38	49.4	190	62.7
Total	226		77		303	

Chi Square Significance = 0.0188
Cramer's V = 0.16193

Amount of Bail

The amount of bail required to be posted may be important because if an accused cannot post that amount, then the accused will remain in jail before trial. More males (N = 100) were released at the stationhouse or after their arraignment on their own recognizance than were required to post some amount of bail (N = 75). Of those males who were required to post bail: 71.4 percent were released at the stationhouse after posting up to a maximum of 150; and, 38.5 percent were released at the stationhouse and/or remained free on bail after posting between $150 and $300 of bail. In contrast, the majority of females were detained at the stationhouse and released after their arraignment, with almost no regard to the amount of bail that was required.

TABLE 2, continued

8.   By: SEX CONTROLLING FOR AMOUNT

$Zero or ROR

	Females		Males		Total	
	No.	%	No.	%	No.	%
Release	9	6.8	52	48.1	61	25.3
Detain	4	3.0	8	7.4	12	5.0
Detain-Release	120	90.2	48	44.4	168	69.7
Total	133		108		241	

Chi Square Significance = 0.0000
Cramer's V = 0.50129

$1-150

	Females		Males		Total	
	No.	%	No.	%	No.	%
Release	2	10.0	5	71.4	7	25.9
Detain	4	20.0	1	14.3	5	18.5
Detain-Release	14	70.0	1	14.3	15	55.6
Total	20		7		27	

Chi Square Significance = 0.0052
Cramer's V = 0.62466

TABLE 2, continued

$151-300

	Females		Males		Total	
	No.	%	No.	%	No.	%
Release	44	31.9	10	38.5	54	32.9
Detain	26	18.8	9	34.6	35	21.3
Detain-Release	68	49.3	7	26.9	75	45.7
Total	138		26		164	

Chi Square Significance = 0.0732
Cramer's V = 0.17856

$301-500

	Females		Males		Total	
	No.	%	No.	%	No.	%
Release	5	3.8	0	0.0	5	3.0
Detain	56	42.4	24	72.7	80	48.5
Detain-Release	71	53.8	9	27.3	80	48.5
Total	132		33		165	

Chi Square Significance = 0.0065
Cramer's V = 0.24714

$501-1000

	Females		Males		Total	
	No.	%	No.	%	No.	%
Release	2	4.3	0	0.0	2	4.1
Detain	13	28.3	2	66.7	15	30.6
Detain-Release	31	67.4	1	33.3	32	65.3
Total	46		3		49	

Chi Square Significance = 0.3702
Cramer's V = 0.20141

Mre $1000

	Females		Males		Total	
	No.	%	No.	%	No.	%
Release	1	4.3	0	0.0	1	3.4
Detain	14	60.9	4	66.7	18	62.1
Detain-Release	8	34.8	2	33.3	10	34.5
Total	23		6		29	

Chi Square Significance = 0.8652
Cramer's V = 0.09992

Attorney

The majority of females who had a public defender represent them (59.6 percent) were not released until after their arraignment; and, the majority of females who retained private counsel (68.1 percent) were also not released until after their arraignment. Likewise, the majority of males who had a public defender appointed to represent them (54.7 percent) were not released until after their arraignment. In contrast, the majority of males who hired a private attorney to represent them (56.1 percent) were released at the stationhouse.

Other Offenses Charged at the Time of the Arrest

Both males and females were more likely to be detained at the stationhouse and released after their arraignment if they were charged with an additional offense. However, 42.1 percent of males released at the stationhouse did not have an additional offense charged against them, while 13.2 percent of females who did not have an additional offense charged were released at the stationhouse.

TABLE 2, continued

9.   By: SEX CONTROLLING FOR ATTORNEY

Public Defender

	Females		Males		Total	
	No.	%	No.	%	No.	%
Release	17	6.3	5	5.8	22	6.1
Detain	93	34.2	34	39.5	127	35.5
Detain-Release	162	59.6	47	54.7	209	58.4
Total	272		86		358	

Chi Square Significance = 0.6651
Cramer's V = 0.04773

Private Attorney

	Females		Males		Total	
	No.	%	No.	%	No.	%
Release	44	21.6	23	56.1	67	27.3
Detain	21	10.3	3	7.3	24	9.8
Detain-Release	139	68.1	15	36.6	154	62.9
Total	204		41		245	

Chi Square Significance = 0.0000
Cramer's V = 0.28996

TABLE 2, continued

10. By: SEX CONTROLLING FOR WHETHER OTHER OFFENSES WERE CHARGED AT THE TIME OF ARREST

No Other Offenses Charged

	Females		Males		Total	
	No.	%	No.	%	No.	%
Release	57	13.2	67	42.1	124	21.0
Detain	103	23.9	43	27.0	146	24.7
Detain-Release	271	62.9	49	30.8	320	54.2
Total	431		159		590	

Chi Square Significance = 0.0000
Cramer's V = 0.34117

Other Offenses Were Charged

	Females		Males		Total	
	No.	%	No.	%	No.	%
Release	7	11.1	0	0.0	7	8.0
Detain	15	23.8	5	20.8	20	23.0
Detain-Release	41	65.1	19	79.2	60	69.0
Total	63		24		87	

Chi Square Significance = 0.1985
Cramer's V = 0.19279

Employment Status

Most males and females who were unemployed were not released until after their arraignment. In particular, 63.1 percent of females and 52.5 percent of males fell into this category. Additionally, 63.6 percent of females who were employed were also not released until after their arraignment. In contrast, 65.0 percent of males who were employed were released at the stationhouse.

Form of Bail

Of those persons who were required to post bail, most males and females could secure release by some form of bail. In particular, 91.6 percent of the males and 86.8 percent of the females who sought their release with cash bail were released at either the stationhouse or after arraignment; 87.5 percent of the males and 98.0 percent of the females who sought their release with an insurance bond were released after their arraignment; and 100.0 percent of the males and 87.9 percent of the females who utilized some form of a surety bond were able to secure their release before trial. In addition, for those that were not released, judges allowed the accused a great flexibility in finding a form of bail which could aid the accused in securing pretrial release. Therefore, it does appear as though the form of bail required posed any undue hardship on persons who sought pretrial release.

TABLE 2, continued

11. By: SEX CONTROLLING FOR EMPLOYMENT STATUS

Unemployed

	Females		Males		Total	
	No.	%	No.	%	No.	%
Release	48	12.6	6	7.5	54	11.7
Detain	93	24.3	32	40.0	125	27.1
Detain-Release	241	63.1	42	52.5	283	61.3
Total	382		80		462	

Chi Square Significance = 0.0132
Cramer's V = 0.13686

Employed

	Females		Males		Total	
	No.	%	No.	%	No.	%
Release	2	18.2	52	65.0	54	59.3
Detain	2	18.2	9	11.3	11	12.1
Detain-Release	7	63.6	19	23.8	26	28.6
Total	11		80		91	

Chi Square Significance = 0.0094
Cramer's V = 0.32039

12. By: SEX CONTROLLING FOR FORM OF BAIL

None

	Females		Males		Total	
	No.	%	No.	%	No.	%
Release	18	12.7	53	48.6	71	28.3
Detain	4	2.8	8	7.3	12	4.8
Detain-Release	120	84.5	48	44.0	168	66.9
Total	142		109		251	

Chi Square Significance = 0.0000
Cramer's V = 0.42763

TABLE 2, continued

Cash

	Females		Males		Total	
	No.	%	No.	%	No.	%
Release	39	36.8	14	58.3	53	40.8
Detain	14	13.2	2	8.3	16	12.3
Detain-Release	53	50.0	8	33.3	61	46.9
Total	106		24		130	

Chi Square Significance = 0.1523
Cramer's V = 0.17015

Insurance Bond

	Females		Males		Total	
	No.	%	No.	%	No.	%
Release	2	2.0	0	0.0	2	1.8
Detain	0	0.0	1	12.5	1	0.9
Detain-Release	99	98.0	7	87.5	106	97.2
Total	101		8		109	

Chi Square Significance = 0.0016
Cramer's V = 0.34359

Suretys

	Females		Males		Total	
	No.	%	No.	%	No.	%
Release	4	12.1	0	0.0	4	11.1
Detain	0	0.0	0	0.0	0	0.0
Detain-Release	29	87.9	3	100.0	32	88.9
Total	33		3		36	

Chi Square Significance (raw) = 0.5224; corrected = 1.0000
Phi = 0.10660

Combination (cash, insurance bond, surety)

	Females		Males		Total	
	No.	%	No.	%	No.	%
Release	1	1.1	0	0.0	1	0.8
Detain	84	90.3	31	93.9	115	91.3
Detain-Release	8	8.6	2	6.1	10	7.9
Total	93		33		126	

Chi Square Significance = 0.7453
Cramer's V = 0.06831

EVALUATION OF FINDINGS

Prostitution and patronizing a prostitute both originated from New York's vagrancy statute. When the state decided to revise its criminal code, prostitution offenses were separated from the vagrancy offense. In 1967, prostitution was classified as a class B misdemeanor and patronizing was classified as a violation (a less serious offense). Due to pressure placed on the state legislature from women's groups, patronizing was upgraded to a class B misdemeanor in September, 1978.[29] For approximately the first one and one-half years covered by this study, patronizing was not as severe an offense as prostitution, while, for the remaining one and one-half years, the two offenses were of equal legal severity.

The results of this study indicate that over the three-year period, 1977-1979, persons arrested for patronizing began to be treated in the same manner as persons arrested for prostitution. That is, in 1979, most of those arrested for patronizing were *not* released after their arrest, while the majority of those arrested for patronizing in 1977 *were* released after their arrest. On the basis of these figures alone, it appears that when the legislature defined patronizing to be as severe an offense as prostitution, males were more likely to be treated in the same fashion as females. However, even though the number of males who were both arrested for patronizing and released at the stationhouse decreased, the data still shows a consistent gender difference in pretrial release status; females were more likely to be detained than males.

Goldkamp found a similar result when he studied bail decisions.[30] In order to assess which variables affected a defendant's pretrial release status, Goldkamp performed a Predictive Attribute Analysis (PAA) on data that he had collected in Philadelphia, Pennsylvania.[31] The results of the PAA indicated that ''the more seriously charged a defendant is and the greater indications of prior or pending involvement with the criminal process, the greater the likelihood of pretrial detention.''[32] Community ties variables, in his study, did not prove to be indicators of pretrial release status, although race and income were to ''*some extent concomitants of high rates of detention.*''[33] Thus, when judges made decisions about an accused's pretrial release status, they utilized ''traditional decisions criteria'' (i.e., severity of the criminal charge) which circumvented the state's bail reform efforts.[34]

While Goldkamp's ''severity of offense'' rationale might explain the change in the pretrial release status of those arrested for patronizing, an alternative explanation exists. The explanation concerns the city of Buffalo's efforts to revitalize its hard-hit economy. Buffalo is a city with one of the highest unemployment rates in the nation, as it is affected heavily by runaway shops and by steel and automobile industry plant closings and layoffs. In order to turn the economic condition of the city around, the city's mayor and other community leaders have been attempting to steer the city away from its dependency on industry and towards tourism and consumerism. The city has built a convention center,[35] developed a theatre district,[36] started building a new mass transit system,[37] has provided funds to refurbish the downtown area,[38] has encouraged the building of hotels and new downtown apartments,[39] and has stepped up its efforts to curtail prostitution in the downtown area.[40] Prostitution activity came under attack primarily because it is believed to detract from the city's downtown image and to adversely affect property values.[41] Business groups have been especially active in pressuring the police department to "clean up the streets" of prostitution.[42] One method that the city devised for eliminating prostitution was "Operation Johnny." Captain Kennedy, of the Buffalo Vice Squad, has been a key figure in the city's efforts to curtail prostitution. Captain Kennedy indicated that "Operation Johnny" was a method to stop prostitution because it was designed to take the profit out of prostitution by arresting patrons, and, thus, stopping the "flow of cash." In particular, he stated that by deterring the patron, prostitution, and the crime that it causes, would be cut down.[43] Of particular importance, then, is the fact that much of the change in the patron arrest practices has not been due to the change in the law, but a change in police policy within the city.[44]

In addition to the change in local police policy, another reason which makes the "severity of offense" explanation difficult to accept as the major reason for the change in the patron arrest practices is that prostitution and patronizing are offenses which are socially and culturally defined, particularly along gender-based lines. When pressured by the public to do something about prostitution, police generally respond by arresting female streetwalkers[45] who "represent the low end of the economic scale."[46] In this study, four profiles of accused emerge. The profiles indicate the characteristics of an accused which are most closely associated with a particular pretrial release category and are separated in accordance with the gender of the accused. The profiles create three categories of male defendants and one category of female defendants.

Profile 1. An accused who was most successful in securing pretrial release at the stationhouse had the following description: a male arrested for patronizing; white; over 25 years of age; employed; resided outside the city limits (suburbs or other areas); hired a private attorney to represent him; was not charged with additional offenses at the time of the arrest; and, was not required to post bail, or was required to post a low bail amount.

Profile 2. An accused who was most successful in securing pretrial release after arraignment was a female arrested for prostitution, regardless of: residence; age; bail amount; attorney; employment status; or whether another offense was charged against her at the time of the arrest.

Profile 3. An accused who was often successful in securing pretrial release after arraignment was a male arrested for prostitution; aged 20 to 24 years; who resided within the city limits; posted a low bail amount; had a public defender assigned; and was unemployed.

Profile 4. Finally, although most defendants were successful in securing their release at some point of time before their trial, an accused who was most likely to be unsuccessful in securing release had the following description: a male arrested for prostitution; black; aged 15 to 19 years; who was required to post bail that was over $300; unemployed; and was not charged with any additional offenses at the time of the arrest.

The profiles show, rather clearly, that the differences, between the categories of defendants and their pretrial release status, can be explained by gender, as well as by the offense charged. Additionally, socioeconomic variables, such as race and employment status, appear to influence one's pretrial release status. The profiles are almost stereotypes of patrons and streetwalkers. Thus, male patrons were generally released earlier than prostitutes, and young, black, male prostitutes were the least successful in securing pretrial release. Equal offense severity lessened differences in treatment but did not eliminate gender (and class) based distinctions.

CONCLUSION

This paper discusses the effect of New York's bail reform legislation upon the pretrial release of those accused of a prostitution offense. It was postulated that although the state's bail reform measures were designed to allow a larger number of persons to be released before trial, the legislation did not really alter the pretrial release status of the accused to any significant degree. The paper's hypothesis is that females would not be released as quickly as males arrested for prostitution offenses. In general, the hypothesis was supported by the data. In addition, differences based upon offense, race, income, etc., were shown to exist. Patrons in Buffalo who were employed, white, lived in the city's suburbs, etc., were released more quickly than prostitutes. The patrons' early pretrial release is directly related to the state's legislative policy which allows the police to act in lieu of the arraignment judge. Although, over the three years studied, patrons began to be treated more like prostitutes, this shift probably has more to do with a change in the city's economic conditions and the resulting increased pressure on the police to combat prostitution than the initial difference between the severity of the prostitution and patronizing offenses.

NOTES

1. Forest Dill, "Discretion, Exchange and Social Control: Bail Bondsmen in Criminal Courts," 9 *Law and Society Review* 639 at 641 (1975).

2. N.Y.C.P.L. Article 500 (McKinney's, 1971).

3. N.Y.C.P.L. Article 500 (McKinney's Practice Commentary, 1971).

4. *People ex rel. Schweizer* v. *Welch*, 40 A.D. 2d 621, 336 N.Y.S. 2d 556 (1972); *People* v. *Brown*, 96 Misc. 2d 127, 408 N.Y.S. 2d 927 (1978).

5. N.Y.C.P.L. § 530.20 (McKinney's, 1971).

6. Prostitution and Patronizing a Prostitute are both class B misdemeanors in New York, N.Y.P.L. § § 230.00, 230.03 (McKinney, 1980). Although the state currently creates several categories of the patronizing offense, ranging in degree of seriousness from a class B misdemeanor to a class D felony, the only patronizing arrests which occurred during the time period studied were classified as class B misdemeanors or as violations. Patronizing was upgraded from a violation in September, 1978, N.Y.P.L. § § 230.03-230.06 (McKinney, 1980).

7. N.Y.P.L. § 140.20 (2), (3), (McKinney, 1981).

8. N.Y.P.L. § 170.10 (7) (McKinney, 1971 and 1981-1982 Supp.).

9. N.Y.P.L. § 140.20 (2a) McKinney, 1981). The police may issue to an accused an appearance ticket which instructs the accused to appear in court at a future date, N.Y. C.P.L. § 150.10 (McKinney, 1981).

10. N.Y.C.P.L. § § 140.20, 150,30 (McKinney, 1981). According to N.Y. C.P.L. § 150.30, "Prearraignment bail may be fixed in the following amounts:. . .(b) If the arrest was for a class B misdemeanor. . ., any amount not exceeding two hundred fifty dollars."

11. N.Y.C.P.L. § 140.20 (1) (McKinney, 1981).

12. *People ex rel. Lobell* v. *McDonnell*, 296 N.Y. 109, 71 N.E. 2d 423 (1947); *People ex rel. Paone* v. *Phimister*, 29 N.Y. 2d 580, 324 N.Y.S. 2d 311 (1971); *People* v. *Maldonado*, 95 Misc. 2d 113, 407 N.Y.S. 2d 393 (1978).

13. Both the Constitution (8th amendment) and the New York State Constitution (Article 1 § 5) prohibit the imposition of excessive bail on an accused by a court.

14. N.Y.C.P.L. § 520.10 (McKinney, 1971 and 1982-1983 Supp.).

15. N.Y.C.P.L. § 150.10 (McKinney Practice Commentary, 1981).

16. John Baumann, "The Limits of the Legal Reform: Bail and Systematic Class Oppression," 3 *Research in Law and Sociology* 321 at 338 (1980).

17. Baumann, supra., at 338-339.

18. John Goldkamp and Michael Gottfredson, "Bail Decision Making and Pretrial Detention: Surfacing Judicial Policy," 3 *Law and Human Behavior* 227 at 237 (1979).

19. Goldkamp and Gottfredson, supra., at 240.

20. Goldkamp and Gottfredson, supra., at 238-240.

21. Goldkamp and Gottfredson, supra., at 242-245.

22. *Craig* v. *Boren,* 429 U.S. 190, 97 S. Ct. 451 (1976).

23. For the purposes of this paper, "prostitution activity" is defined as "prostitution" and "patronizing a prostitute." Special thanks is extended to Ms. Lee Gagnon, Director of Buffalo City Court's Record Room, for her help in securing access to court records.

24. The total number of arrests for prostitution activity in Buffalo, N.Y., between 1977 and 1979 is 967, leaving a difference of 158 cases which were not included in the study. There are two reasons for such failure to include: 1) the cases were not closed—Buffalo City Court restricted data collection to cases which reached a final disposition; and, 2) the cases were misfiled and not easily located.

25. Steven Clarke, Jean Freeman and Gary Koch, "Bail Risk: A Multivariate Analysis," 5 *Journal of Legal Studies* 341 at 364, 372 (1976).

26. Clarke et al., supra., at 360-364, 374-375.

27. *Cleveland State Law Review,* "The Prediction of Court Appearance: A Study of Bail in Cleveland," 27 *Cleveland State L.R.* 587 at 601-605 (1978).

28. *Cleveland State L. R.,* supra., at 605-606.

29. N.Y.P.L. § 230 et seq. (McKinneys, 1980).

30. John Goldkamp, *Two Classes of Accused,* Cambridge, Massachusetts, Ballinger (1979).

31. Goldkamp, supra., at 174-175.

32. Goldkamp, supra., at 181.

33. Goldkamp, supra., at 181.

34. Goldkamp, supra., at 224.

35. The Buffalo Evening News, section F April 13, 1980.

36. The Buffalo Courier Express, "Theatre District Face-lift to Begin," page 1, July 14, 1974.

37. The Buffalo Evening News, " 'Traumatic' Tunnel Work is About to Begin," page B-3, August 12, 1979.

38. The Buffalo Courier Express, "Theatre District Face-lift to Begin," page 1, July 14, 1979.

39. The Buffalo Evening News, "Hotel-Office Project to Start in Year," page A-1, September 1, 1979; The Buffalo Courier Express, "Townhouses on the Waterfront," page H-6, September 14, 1980.

40. The Buffalo Courier Express, "Businessmen Say Prostitutes Flooding Allen-Main Area," page 1, March 17, 1980.

41. The Buffalo Courier Express, "Businessmen Say Prostitutes Flooding Allen-Main Area," page 1, March 17, 1980.

42. The Buffalo Courier Express, "New Phase May Buff Away Grime on Chippewa History," page A-1, February 22, 1981; The Buffalo Courier Express, "Chippewa Street Reputation Casts Shadow on Downtown," page B-1, September 7, 1980.

43. Personal interview with Captain Kennedy, Commander of Buffalo vice squad, Fall 1979.

44. Personal interview with Chief Ford, Erie County Sheriff's Department, Summer 1979.

45. Francis Bernat, "Selective Enforcement and the New York State Prostitution Statute," (unpublished manuscript, 1982).

46. Samuel Walker, *The Police in America*, New York, New York, McGraw-Hill (1983), at 145.

REFERENCES

Baumann, J. 1980. The limits of legal reform: Bail and systematic class oppression. *Research in Law and Sociology, 3*, 321-344.

Bernat, F. Selective enforcement and the New York State prostitution statute (unpublished, 1982.)

Bidden, J. 1981. Reducing crime and detention through pretrial services. *Trial, 17*, 31-33.

The Buffalo Courier Express. July 14, 1979 "Theatre District Face-lift to Begin," page 1.

_____. September 7, 1980 "Chippewa Street Reputation Casts Shadow on Downtown," page B-1.

_____. September 14, 1980 "Townhouses on the Waterfront," page H-6.

_____. February 22, 1981 "New Phase May Buff Away Grime on Chippewa History," page A-1.

_____. March 17, 1981 "Businessmen Say Prostitutes Flooding Allen-Main Area," page 1.

The Buffalo Evening News. August 12, 1979 " 'Traumatic' Tunnel Work is About to Begin," page B-3.

_____. April 13, 1980 Section F

_____. September 1, 1979 "Hotel-Office Project to Start in Year," page A-1.

Clarke, S., Freeman, J., Koch, G. "Bail Risk: A Multivariate Analysis." 5 *Journal of Legal Studies* 341-385.

Cleveland State L. R. 1978. The prediction of court appearance: A study of bail in Cleveland. *Cleveland State L. R., 27*, 587-617.

Columbia Journal of Law and Social Problems. 1973. An answer to the problem of bail: A proposal in need of emprical confirmation. *Columbia J. of Law and Soc. Problems, 9*, 394-441.

Columbia Law Review. 1982. The eighth amendment and the right to bail: Historical perspectives. *Columbia L. R., 82*, 328-362.

Dill, F. 1975. Discretion, Exchange and Social Control: Bail Bondsmen in Criminal Courts. *Law and Society Review, 9*, 639-674.

Goldkamp, J. 1979. *Two classes of accused.* Cambridge, Massachusetts; Ballinger.

Goldkamp, J., and Gottfredson, M., 1979. Bail decision making and pretrial detention: Surfacing judicial policy. *Law and Human Behavior, 3*, 227-249.

Nagel, S., and Neef, M., 1976. Bail, not jail, for more defendants. *Judicature, 60*, 172-198.

Tennessee Law Review. 1978. Constitutional law—Equal protection—Imposing money bail. *Tennessee L. R., 46*, 203-221.

Walker, S. 1983. *The police in America.* New York, New York: McGraw-Hill.

Washburn Law Journal. 1977. Constitutional law: Equal protection for indigents in the bail system. *Washburn L. J., 17*, 648-656.

Wheeler, G., and Wheeler, C., 1982. Bail reform in the 1980's: A response to the critics. *Criminal Law Bulletin, 18*, 228-240.

The Female Offender's Adjustment to Prison Life: A Comparison of Psychodidactic and Traditional Supportive Approaches to Treatment

Faye E. Sultan
Gary T. Long
Stephan A. Kiefer
David M. Schrum
James W. Selby
Lawrence G. Calhoun

ABSTRACT. Sixty-one female inmates of the North Carolina Correctional Center for Women participated in a 3-week treatment study designed to assess the most effective strategy for facilitating adjustment to prison. All subjects were assigned to one of three conditions: (1) a no-treatment Control group, (2) a Support-Only group, or (3) a Psychodidactic Intervention Support group. Subjects in the two treatment groups evidenced a greater level of adjustment than did the control group subjects on two of the four major outcome measures. Implications of these findings were discussed.

The entry of a woman into a correctional facility typically brings with it a period of fear, confusion, and intense psychological upheaval. Suddenly separated from family, friends and familiar

Drs. Sultan, Long, Selby, and Calhoun all have PhDs in Psychology and hold positions on the Psychology Department faculty at The University of North Carolina at Charlotte. Mr. Kiefer and Mr. Schrum have Masters Degrees in Psychology and hold positions on the mental health staff at the North Carolina Correctional Center for Women. Dr. Sultan is a consultant to the North Carolina Correctional Center for Women.

Requests for reprints should be sent to Faye E. Sultan, PhD, Department of Psychology, University of North Carolina at Charlotte, Charlotte, NC 28223.

This study was funded by the UNCC Foundation, 1983.

surroundings, the female offender must cope with a new world, a new society about which she knows very little. Prison rules, expectations of staff and other inmates, lack of privacy, and sexual intimidation all confront the new inmate.

Little systematic attention has been paid to developing programs specifically designed to facilitate adjustment to prison life, despite the general acknowledgement of the correctional/psychological staff of correctional facilities that the early days of incarceration represent a highly stressful period. While many investigations have addressed other aspects of female incarceration, i.e., pre-release training (Adler, 1981; Fine, 1978; Herman, 1979; Hoffman, 1980; Ketterling, 1970; Lambert, 1976; Sorenson, 1981), there is an unfortunate absence of published research focusing on the adjustment of women to prison. Some correctional facilities may, in fact, be conducting informal intervention programs in this area. This study was an attempt to initiate investigation of an intervention program which might serve to facilitate the entry of women into correctional facilities.

THE PSYCHODIDACTIC MODEL

The therapeutic value of providing personally relevant information to a client in a stressful situation has been demonstrated in a variety of contexts. Didactic components have been included in successful interventions for a variety of problem situations (Calhoun, Selby, and Calhoun, 1983; Sabota and Cappas, 1979). Conveying relevant information within an appropriate professional context has been referred to as psychodidactics (Selby and Calhoun, 1980). Information about the psychological and social changes accompanying a particular problem situation may be a highly effective addition to any therapeutic strategy. Selby and Calhoun (1980) pointed out that such personally relevant information helps to provide a better cognitive framework for the client to interpret her/his own personal experiences. Bandura (1977) emphasizes the importance of such a cognitive framework in helping to shape outcome expectancies. Providing clear information may lead to a reduction of the client's uncertainty, providing a better basis for decision-making, and a more positive outlook.

The basic group psychodidactic program is structured and time-limited. The role of the therapist includes the following: (a) to promote a supportive group atmosphere, (b) to convey relevant information (such as prison rules and social norms) in a timely and appropriate manner, and (c) to help group members to relate that information to their personal and collective experiences.

It was hypothesized that within the prison context, the psychodidactic approach would be particularly useful. The highly predictable period of crisis which each offender faces with her entry into the correctional facility brings with it a series of predictable sources of stress which are easily specified. Thus, in addition to supplying the new inmate with traditional group therapy support, it was hypothesized that the provision of highly personally relevant information would serve to ease the transition into prison life.

METHOD

Subjects

Sixty-one inmates admitted to the North Carolina Correctional Center for Women during July and August, 1983 served as subjects. The mean age for subjects was 26.8 years. Thirty-four of the women were non-white and 27 were white. Fifty-two of the 61 subjects were single, divorced, or widowed; 9 were married or in a marriage-like relationship; and 38 have at least one child. Forty-five of the women were first offenders, while 16 had served one or more previous prison sentences. (For further demographic information, see Table 1.)

Subjects group selection. All new admittees during the treatment period were asked to participate in a short-term "orientation program" designed to improve their adjustment to prison life. Over 90% agreed to complete the questionnaires described below. Subjects were randomly assigned to one of three groups: (1) the Psychodidactic Intervention Support Group, (2) the Support group without any explicit psychodidactic component, or (3) the Control group. Three groups of each type were conducted, one beginning approximately every 72 hours.

Experimental Groups

Support group without an explicit psychodidactic component. The fundamentals of traditional supportive group intervention were the exclusive focus here. The leaders (a psychologist and an inmate

Table 1

Demographic Characteristics of All Participants (N = 61)

Characteristic	Mean
Age	26.8 years
Years of Education	10.7
Race, Caucasian	44%
Race, Black	49%
Race, Other	7%
Unmarried	85%
Married or Cohabiting	15%
Had Job Prior to Incarceration	47%
Served at Least One Previous Prison Sentence	26%

Abuse	Percentage Reporting Abuse
Sexually Abused as Child	16.7%
Physically Abused as Child	25.4%
Sexually Abused as Adult	20.0%
Physically Abused as Adult	58.3%

consultant) facilitated discussion without any explicit presentation of information. Topic areas, those issues which were expected to be of most relevance to the entering inmate, were suggested.

Psychodidactic intervention program. In addition to the process described above, these groups contained an explicit psychodidactic component. Information about specific areas of stress common to the new inmate was provided in didactic form, as well as detailed coping strategies. Each group member was encouraged to relate the material presented to her individual circumstances and to integrate that information in a personally-relevant way.

Measures

Expectancy rating form. This form consists of a seven-point Likert-type scale on which subjects indicated their expectancy of increased psychological adjustment to prison life through participation in the "orientation" programs. Subjects completed this form after they had been provided with a description of the treatment program in which they would participate. Ratings of anticipated gain range from (1) not at all to (7) great improvement.

Background information. This form includes a total of 13 questions to assess offender status and gather demographic data. Specifically, subjects were asked to respond to questions regarding their age, education, ethnic/racial background, marital status, number of children, employment history, previous prison terms, and history of physical/sexual abuse both as children and as adults.

Beck Depression Inventory (BDI). This 21-item scale (1967) is designed to reflect present mood. The scale is completed by having the subject rate each item according to how s/he feels "right now."

Prison Adjustment Questionnaire (PAQ). This 13-item scale addresses three areas of adjusting to prison life: (1) social/emotional functioning, (2) psychosomatic functioning (physical complaints), and (3) for smokers only, level of smoking.

Spielberger State-Trait Anxiety Scale (1968). This 40-item questionnaire is designed to assess both immediate and long-term levels of anxiety.

Procedure

Two inmate consultants (long-time prison residents selected by the principal investigator), the administrative/psychological staff of the North Carolina Correctional Center for Women (NCCW), and the principle investigator participated in a series of three planning meetings prior to the recruitment of subjects and the beginning of the orientation programs. These meetings served to generate ideas about the psychological/situational issues of greatest relevance to the entering inmate at NCCW. Didactic presentations for the psychodidactic groups were prepared.

All subjects completed the pretest questionnaires within 72 hours of their admission to NCCW. Subjects, after having been assigned to their groups, were brought to an air-conditioned testing room by the group facilitators. The entire battery of questionnaires required approximately one hour to complete. These questionnaires were re-administered to all subjects three weeks later utilizing the same procedure.

Immediately following the pretest, subjects assigned to the two experimental (treatment) groups began the treatment component.

These subjects participated in six one-hour sessions facilitated by a psychologist and an inmate consultant. The groups met twice weekly for a three-week period.

RESULTS

Analyses of variance on each of the pretest and the posttest measures indicated one significant difference between the Psychodidactic and the Support conditions. This difference was in their expected benefit from the treatment program. The Psychodidactic group indicated greater expected benefit from the "orientation program" than the Support-Only group (means = 5.9 vs 4.5, $p < .05$). Since this was the only difference and was not an outcome measure, the two treatment groups were combined for statistical comparisons with the control condition to ascertain posttest effects on the four outcome measures.

The measure of psychosomatic functioning (physical symptoms) indicated that, after treatment, the treatment group reported a lower level of physical complaints that were likely to be of psychosomatic origin (p < .04, see Table 2) than did the control group. The treatment group scored lower on the Beck Depression Inventory after treatment than the control group but the difference was not quite reliable statistically (p <.13). There were no differences on the groups' scores on the other two outcome measures as shown in Table 2.

Table 2

Posttest Group Means for Outcome Measures

Outcome Measure	Treatment Group	Control Group	Significance
Beck Depression Inventory	10.9	14.9	p <.13
Speilberger State Anxiety Scale	48.9	48.1	n. s.
Prison Adjustment Questionnaire Social/Emotional Factor	23.8	23.4	n. s.
Prison Adjustment Questionnaire Somatic Complaints Factor	12.5	14.4	p <.04

DISCUSSION

This study was an attempt to systematically evaluate a treatment program designed to aid the female inmate in her adjustment to prison life. Two treatment programs (a Psychodidactic group and a Support Only group) were compared with each other and with a control group to determine the effectiveness of the treatment strategies. Several noteworthy findings resulted.

It was interesting to note that a brief description of the intended treatment methods created a difference in the inmates' expected benefits from treatment even though there were no differences between treatment groups in the outcome measures at posttest. Subjects in the Psychodidactic group expected to benefit more than members of the Support Only group.

Members of all three subject groups indicated a high level of psychosomatic symptomatology in the first few days of their incarceration. At the conclusion of the treatment period, subjects in the two experimental groups reported a significant decrease in this dimension compared to the control group. This suggests that the inmates opportunity to discuss their feelings and share relevant information about their early days in prison was related to a decrease in the number of physical complaints. This finding fits well into the current medical view that somatic symptoms can be reduced by psychological intervention.

Interestingly, there were no significant differences between the two treatment groups following the six-session treatment period. Perhaps the outcome measures were not sensitive enough to detect changes which actually did exist. Or, perhaps, a larger subject sample would better reveal such differences. Further research would certainly help to clarify and/or substantiate the results presented here. Perhaps, however, an alternate explanation for this phenomenon should be considered.

Each set of group facilitators reported that they observed a series of behaviors in their groups which may have made the two distinct treatment methods quite similar in very important ways. As described in the Method section, in the Psychodidactic groups, both a supportive environment and information relevant to inmate concerns were provided. In the Support groups, the provision of specific information was not included. It became clear, however, that such information is truly vital to the new inmate, so vital that certain inmates actually took the "facilitator" role in the Support Only groups. Specifically, first offenders seemed to "appoint" one or two of the recidivists, the repeat offenders and treat these women as they did the facilitators in the Psychodidactic groups. These more experienced inmates were asked specific questions about prison life, and, in fact, eventually discussed most of the topics addressed by the Psychodidactic group facilitators. A large amount of "personally relevant information," the essential component of the psychodidactic treatment, was therefore, communicated to the Support Only group members. Further, it is possible that such discussion took place even in the Control group situation, accounting for the relative lack of significant findings.

This study is clearly a preliminary investigation. The complex life situation of the female offender has only recently become the subject of empirical study. Future research will serve to clarify both the psychological/emotional needs of the incarcerated woman and the strategies which are most effective in meeting her needs.

REFERENCES

Adler, F. (Ed.) *The incidence of female criminality in the contemporary world.* New York: New York University Press, 1981.

Bandura, A. *Social learning theory.* New Jersey: Prentice-Hall, Inc., 1977.

Beck, A. T. *Depression: Clinical, experimental and theoretical aspects.* New York: Harper, 1967.

Calhoun, L. G., Selby, J. W., & Calhoun, M. L. The psychological value of prepared child-birth. In J. W. Selby, L. G. Calhoun, A. E. Vogel, & H. E. King (Eds.) *Psychology and human reproduction.* New York: The Free Press, 1980.

Fine, J. An exploratory study to measure the post release effectiveness of work-training release programs. *Offender Rehabilitation,* 1978, *2,* 215-224.

Herman, A. M. If she were a carpenter—Non-traditional apprenticeships for women in prison. *Corrections Today,* 1979, *41,* 24-25.

Hoffman, K. S. Variables relating to program outcomes in a community-based program for women offenders. *Dissertation Abstracts International,* 1980, *40* (11-A), 6016.

Ketterling, M. E. Rehabilitating women in jail. *Journal of Rehabilitation,* 1970, *36,* 36-38.

Lambert, L. R., & Madden, P. G. The adult female offender: The road from institution to community life. *Canadian Journal of Criminology and Corrections,* 1967, *18,* 319-331.

Selby, J. W., & Calhoun, L. G. Psychodidactics: An undervalued and underdeveloped treatment tool of psychological intervention. *Professional Psychology,* 1980, *11,* 236-241.

Sobota, W. L., & Cappas, A. T. Semantic differential changes associated with participation in a public lecture series describing the emotional and behavioral consequences of divorce. *Journal of Divorce,* 1979, *3,* 137-151.

Sorenson, V. Educational and vocational needs of women in prison. *Corrections Today,* 1981, *43,* 61-67.

Spielberger, C. D., Gorsuch, R. L., & Lushene, R. E. *The state-trait anxiety inventory. Preliminary test manual for Form X.* Tallahassee, FL: Florida State University, 1968.

Evidence of Unidimensionality of Locus of Control in Women Prisoners: Implications for Prisoner Rehabilitation

James Griffith

ABSTRACT. Expectancy for locus of control of reinforcement (LOC) was originally conceived as being a unidimensional construct. Results from recent studies employing samples from varied populations have generally shown LOC to be multidimensional, that there are two distinct types of externals: those who perceive reinforcement as determined by chance factors and those who perceive reinforcement as controlled by powerful others. The purpose of the present study was to investigate the dimensionality of the LOC construct in a prison sample. Given the nature of control in prisons, the dimensionality of LOC was expected to show variation. The Levenson (1972) multidimensional LOC measure was administered to a sample of volunteers ($n = 174$) from randomly selected inmates at a state prison for women in the Western United States. Unlike past factor analytic studies which showed items to load on three factors, factor analyses of data obtained from the present sample showed the presence of one factor, the internal-external dimension. Furthermore, the dimensionality of LOC was unrelated to length of imprisonment. Homogeneity of sex, race, and socioeconomic status perhaps best explain results. Implications for prisoner rehabilitation involving manipulation of inmate perception of control for reinforcement are discussed.

Rotter (1966) developed a scale to measure the degree to which a person perceived reinforcements as the result of one's own actions (referred to as internal control) as opposed to forces outside of one's control (referred to as external control). This psychological construct, called locus of control (LOC), was conceived as being unidi-

James Griffith, PhD, is Assistant Professor and Research Psychologist in the Department of Psychology at California State University-Los Angeles, Los Angeles, CA. His mailing address for reprint information is 118 West Tenth Street, Claremont, CA 91711.

Views and opinions expressed in this paper are solely those of the author and do not necessarily reflect the views and opinions of any state or federal Department of Corrections.

mensional with internal control at one endpoint and external control at the opposite endpoint. However, results from factor analyses of responses to the Rotter I-E (Internal-External) LOC scale have generally shown the LOC construct to be multidimensional rather than unidimensional (Collins, 1974; Mirels, 1970; Zuckerman & Gerbasi, 1977).

In view of the accumulating evidence pointing to the multidimensionality of the LOC construct, Levenson (1972) developed a scale whereby two aspects of externality could be obtained: belief in control of reinforcement by powerful others and belief in chance or fate controlling reinforcement. Her third dimension was belief in personal control. The construction of the Levenson scale was theoretically based, though results from several factor analytic studies have empirically attested her tripartite conception (Levenson, 1973, 1974). In addition, persons who perceived their lives as controlled by powerful others have been shown to be behaviorally and cognitively different from those who perceived fate or chance controlling their lives (Levenson & Miller, 1976; Prociuk & Breen, 1974, 1975).

More recent factor analytic studies of data obtained from large samples of Marine Corps recruits ($n = 2648$) (Vickers, Conway, & Haight, 1981a; Vickers, Conway, Haight, & Butler, 1981b) and U.S. Navy men ($n = 914$) (Butler & Burr, 1980) also showed the presence of the Levenson LOC dimensions. In the Vickers et al. study (1981b) comparisons were also made between factor structures of different ethnic/racial groups. Noteworthy is that one general factor emerged in the Hispanic sample.

Evidence from other investigations suggests that factor structure and the dimensionality of LOC are dependent on the population being sampled. For example, Gurin, Gurin, Lao, and Beattie (1969) found black Americans to respond to the Rotter I-E LOC scale in terms of whether or not items reflected control *in their personal* lives and control in people's lives *in general.* This separation of control found in blacks (i.e., what applies to oneself and one's life, and what applies to the general population) was atypical of results obtained from white Americans. Gurin et al. posited thàt the difference in LOC between the two ethnic groups was attributable to differences in the life experiences of black and white Americans; the general American ideology of personal controllability (Levenson, 1981, pp. 19-21) was oftentimes inconsistent with the life experiences of black Americans. Greater uncertainties were associated with the lives of black Americans than those of white Americans, and consequently, blacks developed an attitude of control reflective of their life situation in addition to the sociocultural norm of control. Results from yet another study suggest that the factor structure of LOC is somewhat dependent on the population being studied. For example, Nagelschmidt and Jakob (1977) factor analyzed responses to the Rotter I-E LOC scale given by 170 Brazilian women. Analyses yielded two factors: belief in control over personal relations, and belief in the inability to change the course of certain world happenings. The former factor was interpreted as essentially tapping the original Rotter I-E dimension, and the latter, as measuring a sociocultural attitude of fatalism. The difference in the factor structure in relation to those found in earlier studies, researchers explained, was attributable to the characteristics of the population being studied: The sample was largely comprised of the underprivileged, characterized by their fatalistic ideology toward life, though recent exposure to technological advances had fostered a sense of personal efficacy.

Prison environments are noted for their stringent control over inmates; inmate activities are continually observed and regulated by members of the prison staff (see Ward & Kassebaum, 1965). To enhance prison security, capricious and random behaviors of prison staff members toward inmates are often encouraged (e.g., periodic mail censorship, telephone conversation monitoring, and personal and room searches). The prisoner subculture also influences inmate behavioral and psychological adjustment. The prisoner culture imposes strong controls on behaviors of inmates, such as defining one's standing within the inmate social hierarchy, the way an inmate is to behave with other inmates and the prison staff, and even one's sexuality (Bowker, 1977). The inmate "code of behavior" is often implicit, requiring experimentation on the part of new arrivals to test limits of acceptable behavior. Rewards and sanctions are given by fellow inmates to induce normative prisoner behavior (Bowker, 1977, pp. 14-16), and this learning process undoubtedly affects an inmate's generalized expectancy for control of reinforcement.

Crises and situations in which outcomes are perceived as uncontrollable (as when one first enters prison and is unaware of reward contingencies) have been associated with shifts toward externality (Gorman, 1968; McArthur, 1970; Smith, 1970). Given the nature of control in prisons and the prisoner subculture, it is reasonable to expect LOC of prison inmates to undergo some changes. Indeed, findings of studies (Kiehlbauch, 1968; Lefcourt & Ladwig, 1966; Levenson, 1975) seem to suggest this: externality covaried significantly and positively with length of imprisonment. Yet, no study has explored the dimensionality of LOC in a sample of prison inmates. What underscores the importance of this study is that expectancy for control of reinforcement has implications for prisoner adjustment, learning potential, and rehabilitation. Both mild and severe forms of psychopathology have been positively correlated with Levenson's external dimensions (Levenson, 1973; Morelli, Krotinger, & Moore, 1979). Internals, having the perception that rewards and punishments are based on individual behavioral performance, would be expected to be better learners in traditional learning settings, that is, in situations where reinforcement is contingent on personal initiative. Results from several laboratory studies have supported this contention (Logsdon, Bourgeois, & Levenson, 1978; Wagner, Bourgeois, & Levenson, 1974). Studies examining the relationships between LOC and adjustment, and between LOC and learning have shown distinct differences for persons ascribing to Levenson's two aspects of externality. This strongly suggests that separating out these two external orientations is critical in understanding processes of adjustment and learning, and for prisoners, understanding processes of rehabilitation in inmates ascribing to different external orientations. The purpose of this study was then to investigate the dimensionality of LOC in a sample of women prisoners.

METHOD

Subjects

A sample of women inmate volunteers was obtained from a randomly selected sample of 492 inmates at a state prison for women in the Western United States. Selection of the random sample was based on room numbers of rooms in which inmates lived. For each of twelve living units, inmates living in the rooms of randomly selected numbers were requested by way of an institutional pass system to report to a testing room. A total of 196 inmates responded (response rate, 40%); 22 inmates declined to participate in the study.

Procedures

Members of the research team briefly explained the nature of the study to inmates. Participation was made voluntary, and inmates were informed that their responses would remain anonymous. Inmates were then requested to complete the Levenson (1972) IPC Scale. The IPC Scale consists of 24 attitude statements which are keyed to three subscales: Internal (I), Powerful Others (P), and Chance (C). Each statement was rated on a Likert 6-point scale from "strongly disagree (1)" to "strongly agree (6)." High scores indicated general agreement with the subscale orientation. All three subscales showed moderate internal consistency: Cronbach's alpha coefficients for the Internal, Powerful Others, and Chance subscales were .61, .70, and .67 respectively. Participants were also asked to report personal information, such as level of education, annual income before incarceration, age, ethnicity, and total length of imprisonment to date.

RESULTS

Sample Demographic Characteristics

Mean months imprisoned for the sample was 36.2, ranging from 3 months to just over 26 years. The mean age was 30.1 years. The ethnic composition of inmates in the sample was 37 percent white, 36 percent black, 16 percent Mexican American, and 11 percent nonwhite other. The mean number of years of formal education reported by the inmates was 11.7. Mean age and mean months imprisoned of the sample did not significantly differ from those of the general prison population (respectively, for mean age and mean months imprisoned, $t = 1.53$ and $t = 1.17$). In addition, the proportions of whites and nonwhites were not statistically different from those of the prison population (respectively, for whites and nonwhites, $Z = -.65$ and $Z = .08$).

Mean IPC Scale Scores

The sample mean on the Internal subscale ($M = 38.54$, $SD = 5.62$) was significantly greater than that obtained from a sample of predominately white, lower- to middle-class, female college freshmen and sophomores (Sherman & Ryckman, 1980) (M = 27.01, SD = 5.52; $t(276)$ = 11.83, p <.001). Sample means on the Powerful Others and Chance subscales were respectively 24.04 (SD = 11.21) and 23.15 (SD = 10.56). These were also significantly greater than those obtained in Sherman and Ryckman's sample of women, respectively, M = 14.65, SD = 6.04; M = 15.00, SD = 6.10 ($t(276)$ = 9.03, p <.001 and, $t(276)$ = 8.07, p <.001, respectively).

Factor Analyses of the Levenson IPC Scale

The factor extraction method employed for all subsequent factor analyses was principal components with squared multiple correlations in the diagonals. Components were rotated orthogonally by way of the varimax rotation method.

A factor analysis was conducted on responses given by inmates to the Levenson scale. When factors were unspecified, nine factors emerged with eigenvalues greater than or equal to 1.0. Respectively, factors accounted for 17.6, 10.4, 6.4, 5.6, 5.1, 4.8, 4.7, 4.3, and 4.2 percent of the total variance. Factors were then rotated orthogonally using the varimax method. Items did not load on factors in any interpretable way. A screen test (Cattell, 1966, in Gorsuch, 1974, pp. 152-156) was then done to ascertain the number of interpretable factors and showed the presence of 2 or 3 factors. A three-factor solution was then specified. Factor 1 accounted for 57.8 percent of the variance in the three-factor solution, Factor 2 accounted for 28.9 percent, and Factor 3, 13.3 percent. Factors were then rotated by way of the varimax method. The criterion for an item loading on a factor was ±.30 or greater. Seven of the thirteen items that loaded on Factor 1 were from the Powerful Others subscale, five from the Chance subscale, and one from the Internal subscale. Of the nine items loading on Factor 2, six were from the Internal subscale. The remaining three items were from the Powerful Others and Chance subscales. Three of the five items loading on Factor 3 were from the Chance subscale. The other two items were from the Powerful Others subscale. Four items loaded on more than one factor, and Item 21, "When I get what I want, it's usually because I worked hard for it," failed to load on any of the three factors. Factors 1 and 2, and Factors 2 and 3 were orthogonal (r = −.01 and r = −.10 respectively). The correlation between the two "external LOC" factors, Factors 1 and 3, was substantial ($r = .50$), making the orthogonality of these two latter factors questionable. P and C subscale scores were also observed to be highly correlated ($r = .69$, $p < .001$).

A two-factor solution was then specified to ascertain whether items would load on factors in a more interpretable way. Factor 1 accounted for 66.9 percent of the variance in the two factors. The fifteen items that loaded on Factor 1 were exclusively from the Powerful Others and Chance subscales. Factor 2 accounted for 33.1 percent of the variance in the two-factor solution. Of the eight items that loaded on this factor, seven were from the Internal subscale and one from the Powerful Others subscale. The correlation between these two factors was negligible ($r = -.01$).

Another statistical procedure was performed to ascertain the number of "real" factors present in the IPC scale item rating given by women inmates. Following a rather conservative method described in Nunnally (1967, pp. 357-358), eight factors (one-third the number of variables) were extracted and then rotated using the varimax method. Items with factor loadings $\pm .30$ or greater were used to predict factor scores employing step-wise multiple regression analyses. The cumulative R^2 for Factors 1 through 8 were .51, .36, .69, .43, .33, .30, .23, and .15 respectively. Except for the latter two, all R^2s were significant ($p < .01$). A conservative rule of thumb suggested by Nunnally to determine whether a factor is "real" is if the shrunken R^2 is greater than .50. The shrunken R^2 for only one factor, Factor 3, achieved this criterion. This factor appeared to be the "external" dimension of LOC, but neither clearly Levenson's Powerful Others nor her Chance aspect of external LOC. Of the nine factors that loaded on Factor 3, five items were from the Chance subscale, three items from the Powerful Others subscale, and one item from the Internal subscale. Though the shrunken R^2 of Factor 1 did not reach Nunnally's stringent criterion of .50, Factor 1 had the second highest shrunken R^2 (.43). Factor 1 appeared to be the "internal" dimension of LOC. Of the eight factors that loaded on this factor, six items were from the Internal subscale, and one item each from the Powerful Others and Chance subscales. In summary, the procedure suggested by Nunnally to determine the number of "real" factors showed the presence of one factor, this being the "external" dimension of LOC. At best, this method showed the presence of two factors, the "internal" and "external" dimensions of LOC.

DISCUSSION

Factor analyses of data obtained from the present sample of women prisoners showed inmates responded to only two of the three dimensions of Levenson's LOC scale: external and internal. Such findings are inconsistent with factor analyses of data obtained from nonimprisoned samples (e.g., Butler & Burr, 1980; Levenson, 1973, 1974; Vickers et al., 1981a, 1981b); all of which generally showed the Levenson items to load on their respective factors: internal, powerful others, and chance. There are several post hoc explanations as to why women prisoners differ in the dimensionality of LOC.

Books, television programs (e.g., "Cell Block H"), and motion picture films (e.g., "Brubaker," "Escape from Alcatraz") encourage expectancies of control by "powerful others" in prison. Commonplace are scenes in which inmates are depicted as having little personal freedom and control, and are continually monitored by the ever-present prison guard. Objective aspects of the prison environment undoubtedly promote expectations of control by prison staff. For example, prison guards are highly visible; restricted areas are clearly marked; and movement is controlled by issuance of institutional passes and monitored by electronic devices. A person who has never been to prison and arrives in this environment probably perceives most events as being the result of powerful others (see Kiehlbauch, 1968; Levenson, 1975). Chance events, or events with less discernible origins, may be attributed to the prison system of control or to powerful others within the inmate social hierarchy. This might explain why Powerful Others and Chance subscale items do not load on separate factors.

Another possible explanation as to why factor analyses did not yield three distinct LOC dimensions in the present sample is the nature of behaviors of the prison staff members toward inmates. The most frequently expressed negative experience of the Stanford prison experiment (Haney, Banks, & Zimbardo, 1973) by pseudo-prisoners was the guards' arbitrary and capricious behavior. While on some occasions a simple question of a pseudo-prisoner evoked physical and verbal reprimands, on others, it was given a rational reply. Researchers concluded that "the subjective magnitude of aversiveness was manipulated by the guards not in terms of physical punishment but rather by controlling the psychological dimension of environmental predictability" (p. 96). To the prison inmate then, a seemingly objective chance happening could be perceived as intentional by a capriciously-acting prison staff member. Factor analyses of responses to the Levenson scale for the present sample can be construed as supporting this argument of "misattribution." Such an interpretation, however, relies on inferences which go beyond the data at hand. Post hoc factor analyses of responses to the Levenson scale suggested LOC dimensionality was not related to length of imprisonment. The sample was divided into two subgroups in terms of length of imprisonment already served: short-term imprisoned (16 months or less, $n = 64$) and long-term imprisoned (36 months or more, $n = 63$) women. Factor analyses were then conducted in each subgroup. Items in both subsample analyses loaded on factors similar to that observed in the whole sample. (As the subsample sizes were relatively small, some caution should be exercised in interpreting this analysis.) The sample here was homogeneous in terms of sex, race, and income. The sample was exclusively women, a majority of whom were minorities (63%) and who had reported a relatively low income before incarceration ($M = $11,670$). These demographic similarities might better explain results of factor analyses. Differences in LOC between the sexes, racial groups, and socioeconomic levels are well-documented. Women more often view themselves as less effective in manipulating the environment than do men (Maccoby & Jacklin, 1974). Minority members are generally more external than are majority whites (Jessor, Graves, Hanson, & Jessor, 1968; Lefcourt & Ladwig, 1966). Persons from lower socioeconomic status (SES) are usually more externally oriented than are persons of higher SES (Jessor et al., 1968; Walls & Miller, 1970). These sex, racial, and SES differences in LOC are most often explained in terms of different life events experienced by men and women, by minorities and whites, and by socioeconomically-disadvantaged and advantaged peoples. For example, social expectancies of what constitutes feminine behavior (e.g., passive, dependent, compliant, and submissive) are closely akin to the external orientation of LOC. People of lower SES and minority members more often experience events resulting from actions of powerful others (e.g., denial of work, less educational opportunities) and resulting from chance (e.g., racial discrimination and prejudice). That women prisoners in the current study have difficulty in separating out chance events from those caused by powerful others perhaps that may be best explained by life circumstances unique to their sex, race, and/or SES.

IMPLICATIONS FOR PRISONER REHABILITATION

A crucial aspect of effective learning is that the learner perceives rewards and punishments as a function of his(her) behaviors. Results from several investigations have shown that persons exposed to rewards and punishments outside their personal control view themselves as helpless and suffer from learning deficits (Hiroto & Seligman, 1975; Miller & Seligman, 1976). In most learning situations as in prison rehabilitation, rewards and punishments are dispensed by "powerful others" (e.g., teachers, prison staff members, etc.). Ideally, the learner is expected to develop the perception that his(her) behaviors lead directly to reinforcement and punishment, but equally ideal and perhaps a prerequisite of the former process is when the learner perceives reinforcement as dependent on how well (s)he fulfills the demands of teachers. The least effective learning situation is when the learner views consequences of his (her) behaviors, either rewards or punishments, as capricious and haphazard occurrences (Seligman's [1976] "learned helplessness").

Results obtained in the present study were interpreted as showing prisoner difficulty in separating out behavioral consequences resulting from chance factors and those resulting from intentions of powerful others. Individuals who make a perceptual distinction between outcomes caused by chance and those caused by actions of powerful others have shown greater learning ability than those who do not. Specifically, persons who believe in an unpredictable world in which consequences of personal actions occur haphazardly and randomly think and behave less effectively than do persons who believe in a predictable world in which powerful others control rewards and punishments (Levenson & Miller, 1976; Procuik & Breen, 1974, 1975).

To manage inmates in the short-term and in the long-term rehabilitate inmates, prison staff members issue punishments (e.g., disciplinary documentations) and rewards (e.g., credits which reduce one's sentence term). If, however, inmates perceive such rewards and punishments as independent of their actions (e.g., the result of chance factors, capriciously-acting prison staff members, etc.), then this method will be ineffective in modifying unwanted behaviors and promoting more desirable responses, and may even create in inmates hostile attitudes toward the prison staff. It would appear then an important aspect of prison management and rehabilitation which rely on behavioral learning methods (e.g., California prisons' Work Incentive Program) is cultivating in inmates a perceptual distinction between environmental outcomes that are intentional of prison staff members and those that are chance occurrences. There are, however, some important and provocative considerations for rehabilitative programs which seek to alter one's perceived control of reinforcement. It will be remembered that the sample was comprised of women who were on the whole minorities and who had earned low incomes prior to incarceration. Because of their unique life circumstances, such individuals in the "outside" world could be quite realistic when they perceive consequences of their actions as largely out of their personal control or when they confuse Levenson's external LOC dimensions. If, after incarceration, the inmate is returned to those environments in which behavioral consequences are actually determined by powerful others and/or chance factors, then attempts to change an inmate's perception of control for reinforcement during imprisonment may be more damaging than rehabilitative.

REFERENCES

Bowker, L. H. (1977). *Prisoner subcultures.* Lexington, MA: D. C. Heath.
Butler, M. C., & Burr, R. G. (1980). Utility of the multidimensional locus of control scale in predicting health and job-related outcomes in military environments. *Psychological Reports,* 47, 719-728.
Collins, B. E. (1974). Four components of the Rotter Internal-External Scale: Belief in a difficult world, a just world, a predictable world, and a politically responsive world. *Journal of Personality and Social Psychology,* 29, 381-391.
Gorman, B. S. (1968). An observation of altered locus of control following political disappointment. *Psychological Reports,* 23, 1094.
Gorsuch, R. L. (1974). *Factor analysis.* Philadelphia: Saunders.
Gurin, P., Gurin, G., Lao, R. C., & Beattie, M. (1969). Internal-external control in the motivational dynamics of Negro youth. *Journal of Social Issues,* 25, 29-53.
Haney, C., Banks, W. C., & Zimbardo, P. G. (1973). Interpersonal dynamics in a simulated prison. *International Journal of Criminology and Penology,* 1, 69-97.
Hiroto, D. S., & Seligman, M. E. P. (1975). Generality of learned helplessness in man. *Journal of Personality and Social Psychology,* 31, 311-327.
Jessor, R., Graves, T. D., Hanson, R. C., & Jessor, S. L. (1968). *Society, personality and deviant behavior: A study of a tri-ethnic community.* New York: Holt, Rinehart, & Winston.
Kiehlbauch, J. B. (1968). Selected changes over time in internal-external expectancies in a reformatory population (Doctoral dissertation, Kansas State University, 1968). *Dissertation Abstracts International,* 29, 371B (University Microfilms No. 68-9912).
Lefcourt, H. M., & Ladwig, G. W. (1966). Alienation in Negro and white reformatory inmates. *Journal of Social Psychology,* 68, 153-157.
Levenson, H. (1972). Locus of control and other cognitive correlates of involvement in anti-

pollution activities (Doctoral dissertation, Claremont Graduate School, 1972). *Dissertation Abstracts International, 33,* 5B (University Microfilms No. 72-2325).

Levenson, H. (1973). Multidimensional locus of control in psychiatric patients. *Journal of Consulting and Clinical Psychology, 41,* 397-404.

Levenson, H. (1974). Activism and powerful others. Distinction within the concept of internal-external control. *Journal of Personality Assessment, 38,* 377-383.

Levenson, H. (1975). Multidimensional locus of control in prison inmates. *Journal of Applied Social Psychology, 5,* 342-347.

Levenson, H. (1981). Differentiating among internality, powerful others, and chance. In H. M. Lefcourt (Ed.), *Research with the locus of control construct (Vol. 1): Assessment methods* (pp. 15-63). New York: Academic Press.

Levenson, H., & Miller, J. (1976). Multidimensional locus of control in sociopolitical activists of conservative and liberal ideologies. *Journal of Personality and Social Psychology, 33,* 199-208.

Logsdon, S. A., Bourgeois, A., & Levenson, H. (1978). Locus of control, learned helplessness, and control of heart rate using biofeedback. *Journal of Personality Assessment, 42,* 538-544.

McArthur, L. A. (1970). Luck is alive and well in New Haven: A serendipitous finding on perceived control of reinforcement after the draft lottery. *Journal of Personality and Social Psychology, 16,* 316-318.

Maccoby, E. E., & Jacklin, C. N. (1974). *The psychology of sex differences.* Stanford, CA: Stanford University Press.

Miller, W. R., & Seligman, M. E. P. (1976). Learned helplessness, depression and the perception of reinforcement. *Behaviour Research and Therapy, 14,* 7-17.

Mirels, H. L. (1970). Dimensions of internal versus external control. *Journal of Consulting and Clinical Psychology, 34,* 226-228.

Morelli, G., Krotinger, H., & Moore, S. (1979). Neuroticism and Levenson's locus of control scale. *Psychological Reports, 44,* 153-154.

Nagelschmidt, A. M., & Jakob, R. (1977). Dimensionality of Rotter's I-E Scale in a society in the process of modernization. *Journal of Cross-Cultural Psychology, 8,* 101-112.

Nunnally, J. C. (1967). *Psychometric theory.* New York: McGraw-Hill.

Prociuk, T. J., & Breen, L. J. (1974). Locus of control, study habits and attitudes, and college academic performance. *Journal of Psychology, 88,* 91-95.

Prociuk, T. J., & Breen, L. J. (1975). Defensive externality and its relation to academic performance. *Journal of Personality and Social Psychology, 31,* 549-556.

Rotter, J. B. (1966). Generalized expectancies for internal versus external control reinforcement. *Psychological Monographs, 80*(1, Whole No. 609).

Seligman, M. E. P. (1976). Learned helplessness and depression in animals and man. In J. T. Spence, R. C. Carson, & J. W. Thaibut (Eds.), *Behavioral approaches to therapy.* Morriston, NJ: General Learning Press.

Shearer, R. A., & Moore, J. B. (1978, November). *Personality dimensions of felonious probationers in Texas.* Paper presented at the meeting of the American Society of Criminology, Dallas.

Sherman, M. F., & Ryckman, R. M. (1980). Discriminant validity of Levenson's I and P scales: Used as predictors of causal attribution. *Personality and Social Psychology Bulletin, 6,* 57-62.

Smith, R. E. (1970). Changes in locus of control as a function of life crisis resolution. *Journal of Abnormal Psychology, 75,* 328-332.

Vickers, R. R., Conway, T. L., & Haight, M. A. (1981, April). *Association between Levenson's dimensions of locus of control and measures of coping and defense mechanisms.* Paper presented at the meeting of the Western Psychological Association, Los Angeles. (a)

Vickers, R. R., Conway, T. L., Haight, M. A., & Butler, M. C. (1981, August). *Dimensionality of locus of control in different race groups.* Paper presented at the meeting of the American Psychological Association, Los Angeles. (b)

Wagner, C., Bourgeois, A., & Levenson, H. (1974). Multidimensional locus of control of and voluntary control of GSR. *Perceptual and Motor Skills,* 39, 1142.

Walls, R. T., & Miller, J. J. (1970). Delay of gratification in welfare and rehabilitation clients. *Journal of Counseling Psychology,* 17, 383-384.

Ward, D., & Kassebaum, G. (1965). *Women's prison.* Chicago, IL: Aldine.

Zuckerman, M., & Gerbasi, K. C. (1977). Dimensions of the I-E Scale and their relationship to other personality measures. *Educational and Psychological Measurement,* 37, 159-175.

CB Radio Prostitution: Technology and the Displacement of Deviance

Joan Luxenburg
Lloyd Klein

INTRODUCTION AND BACKGROUND OF THE STUDY

The CB radio has proved its worth to motorists in a variety of ways. These include: warnings of road hazards or speed traps; information, such as directions; calls for assistance, including accidents or disabled vehicles; and, just simply, friendly conversation. It should come as no surprise to us that improved technological means of communication (such as the CB radio) is not limited to law-abiding activities and use. Indeed, the warnings of speed traps (formerly accomplished solely by headlight signals) and the "Smokey and the Bandit" syndrome gave rise to the "outlaw" uses of the CB radio. The CB radio can provide the medium for individuals who wish to conduct deviant business or interactions where mobile communication is desired.

CB radio prostitution represents the displacement of prostitution from the city streets to the interstate highways (Ingle, 1980). However, if one investigates the historical accounts of 19th century America, one finds the "wagon-yard whore" of the interstate post roads.[1] Wagon drivers (the prototype of today's long haul truckers) would stop after a day's ride (drive) at wagon yards (the equivalent of today's interstate rest areas and truck stops) conveniently located along the interstate post roads. There, the wagon drivers could feed and water their horses, bathe themselves, have a meal, etc. Prosti-

Joan Luxenburg is at Central State University, Edmond, OK 73034. Lloyd Klein is at St. John's University, Jamaica, NY 11432.

This paper was presented to the annual meeting of the Academy of Criminal Justice Sciences, March 22-26, 1983, San Antonio, Texas.

tutes would make themselves available in much the same way that "camp followers" made themselves available to soldiers at campsites during the American Civil War. Therefore, highway prostitution has always been with us. The availability of prostitutes at interstate rest areas and truck stops is a functional aspect of the trucker's lifestyle. However, with the popularity of the CB radio, so came a more sophisticated manner of prostitution at these sites.

The rest area or truck stop as a sexual marketplace (without the use of the CB radio) has been recognized by sociologists interested in the study of sociosexual behavior. For instance, Richard R. Troiden (1974) describes male homosexual encounters at a commuter-expressway rest stop in Long Island, New York. (These were not prostitute activities.) The CB radio was apparently not an element of these interactions. The participants signalled each other's interest in sexual engagement by the use of headlights (considered to be in poor taste) and by subtle conversation and/or gestures. Opening pitches included: "Looking for some fun?," "Is there any action around here?," "Looking for excitement?," "Do you play around?," (Troiden, 1974, 212). The rest stop in question had acquired a local reputation for homosexual males and, therefore, had its "regular" visitors. Truckers were not a part of the activity, as the setting was not on a trucking route. Another example of a sociological study of highway sexual encounters (of the nonprostitute variety) was conducted by Jay Corzine and Richard Kirby (1977, 1979) who studied the activity of male homosexuals in a midwestern city in the vicinity of two rest areas and two truck stops located along an interstate highway. Again, no mention of the CB radio was made in this study, as "cruising" by homosexual males toward male truckers was accomplished with either a subtle lowering of one's car window, accompanied by a subtle "Do you have the time?" or a more blatant following of a driver into the rest room and asking if he wants "to get it on" (Corzine and Kirby, 1979, 581). John Zeh conducted an interview of two gay truckers who travelled across the country as trucking partners (The Advocate, 1975). In that journalistic account, the two gay truckers describe their cruising as taking place mostly in gay bars along their trips; although they do acknowledge and partake in the activities of notorious rest areas. Despite these truckers reporting it feasible to visit gay bars, we have found that the peculiarities of the trucker's occupation (e.g., need to remain with the truck; deadlines; etc.) make it hardly likely that heterosexual male truckers will be able to attend bars where they would be able to meet females who are looking for sexual companionship (either paid for or for free). This factor adds to the functional aspect of highway prostitution.

Having established the popularity of highway rest areas and/or truck stops as sexual marketplaces for male homosexuals, it is noteworthy and incumbent upon us to inform the reader that our own initial interest in highway rest areas was for the purpose of studying male homosexual activity. Our "stumbling upon" the female heterosexual prostitution was serendipitous. Our study began in 1979 at "Good Buddy Park," an interstate rest area in Oklahoma. "Good Buddy" is the local CB term for male homosexual. Male homosexual activity dominated Good Buddy Park well before the female heterosexual prostitution began there. However, unlike in the aforementioned studies (e.g., Troiden; Corzine and Kirby), the CB radio was a major factor in sexual cruising. Although the majority of gay males frequenting Good Buddy Park were not announcing themselves over the CB radio, the radio, nevertheless, helped to advertise that location as one for male homosexuals. At approximately the same time that we gained access to a student who was able to systematically tape record CB radio conversations over her (CB radio) home base station, the female prostitutes had all but replaced the male homosexuals. In what may be viewed as an "invasion cycle of neighborhoods," the new group (female prostitutes) had, in fact, "displaced" the male homosexual cruisers. The site retained its name, Good Buddy Park, although some truckers began referring to it as "Dolly Park." Of interest to us is the process whereby a displaced form of prostitution (from streets to highways) actually resulted in displacing another deviant activity (male homosexual cruising) from this particular rest area.

Our analysis focuses upon the former displacement (prostitution from streets to highways) and the consequential modification of the methods of prostitutes and pimps. The efforts of police to control or eliminate the activity requires new strategies. Because our observations of police intervention are not as complete as are our observations of the actual prostitute activity, our analysis here will be limited to a description of CB radio prostitution and pimping.

METHOD

We rely solely upon on-site observations and taped recordings of CB dialogue at one interstate highway rest area and three interstate highway truck stops in Oklahoma. Taped recordings of CB radio dialogue were made by several students enrolled during various semesters (between 1979-1982) in one of the authors' ''individual studies'' courses. For the first two years (1979 and 1980) a female undergraduate student (age 40+) who is a CB enthusiast monitored the radio transmissions from her home base station (either letting the tape run while the radio was on, or while she, herself, was interacting with truckers over the radio. This was done two to three evenings per week (weekends and week nights from 8:00 PM to 2:00 or 3:00 AM). One of the authors routinely visited the rest area (to observe) several evenings per month during 1980 and 1981. When Good Buddy Park was closed in January of 1981, taped recordings became uneventful and, although we listened to CB dialogue for several months later to follow-up on the site's closing, there was no further prostitute activity at the rest area. The activity had moved to three truck stops, one of which was located a few miles south of Good Buddy Park on the same north-south interstate highway. The other two truck stops were on a nearby east-west interstate highway. During the spring of 1981 semester, a male undergraduate student (age 33) covered all three truck stops by on-site observation, taped recordings over his mobile CB radio, interviews with: (1) police (truck stop security guards), (2) the evening managers at the truck stops, and (3) a pimp and prostitute. This student (student #2) occasionally accompanied by one of the authors, followed a schedule similar to student #1's rest area recordings (Student #1 did all her recording in her home, which was located very close to Good Buddy Park.) Therefore, the truck stops were under our observation two to three evenings per week. We did not stay out past midnight, as our work schedules did not permit it. In the fall 1981 semester, student #2 (who had already graduated) volunteered his time to occasionally follow-up on the truck stops (accompanied by one of the authors). It was during the fall 1981 semester that another female student (age 40+) confessed to one of the authors that she was a ''part-time'' CB radio prostitute. (She held a conventional full-time job, and was a full-time undergraduate student.) This student (student #3) allowed one of the authors to accompany her on her highway soliciting. Student #3 avoided the truck stops because of the security guards. She cruised the open highways making her pitches on her CB radio. Student #4, a female undergraduate (age 20+), monitored all three truck stops, accompanied by one of the authors during the fall 1982 semester.

Supplemental to the above activities, we were able to interview several concerned law enforcement officials, e.g., at the Oklahoma

Highway Patrol, Oklahoma State Bureau of Investigation, local Sheriff's office (near Good Buddy Park), and the Oklahoma City Police Department. We were able to observe the "booking room" of one of the truck stops where prostitutes and pimps were photographed and questioned upon arrest. Further, student #2 was able to "tag along" with a pimp and prostitute whom he had befriended. Informal interviews with truckers (who were aware of our study) were conducted; however, these were done for the purpose of having the truckers help us to interpret our data. Further, our interviews with truckers were conducted away from our observational sites. Truckers became available to us through snowball sampling, e.g., announcements made in class that we needed to speak to truckers about CB radio prostitution. Students would refer us to friends and relatives who were truckers, and these respondents, in turn, introduced us to still others who kept the sample snowballing. We never approached truckers at the rest area or truck stops. Neither did we attempt to announce ourselves to prostitutes and pimps. The one exception to the policy of not announcing ourselves to the participants had occurred spontaneously and did work to our advantage. Student #2 did announce himself to a pimp. He gained rapport with the pimp and the pimp's common-law wife (a prostitute), and was able to observe them at work in all activities except for the actual sexual act. Therefore, part of our data is ethnographic. However, since we did not interview other prostitutes and pimps, we recognize the delimitations of our study. Interviewing would have yielded more data. However, we preferred an unobtrusive method of eavesdropping. We chose this method because we were initially interested in pursuing an interactionist perspective, e.g., investigating the types of communication and guidelines for same in CB radio prostitution (Klein and Ingle, 1980a). In view of our method, we stipulate that our study is an impressionistic study. Such studies, although not as fully controlled as other types of designs, can, nevertheless, yield important descriptive data (Horton and Hunt, 1976; 25-26).

FINDINGS

We have analyzed CB radio prostitution as a relatively new form of prostitution, and yet, we recognize it as a modified version of an old form of prostitution (wagon-yard prostitution of 19th century America). With the aid of the CB radio, truckers and prostitutes make their desires known over the air waves. Examples of dialogue (opening pitches, etc.), ranging from the subtle to the very abrasive, are provided here (Ingle, 1980, 1-6):

> *Prostitute:* "Yeah, how about this Mr. 18-Wheeler going down the highway? Would you like to have some fun? Ah, anybody like to see a Beaver tonight? You got the (Handle). Come on, talk to me. Come on, one of you horny truck drivers out there. Would you like to see a Beaver tonight?"

> *Driver:* "(Handle), you're too damn high."

> *Prostitute:* "Ah, well, hell, maybe next time. You just save your quarters and dimes and maybe sometime we can date."

> *Prostitute:* "Would one of you buffaloes out there like to see a Beaver? Been waitin' for a stampede. Come on. Aw, now come on drivers. Come on and get some of this good pussy we got out here. You got the (Handle). Come on and get some of my pussy. You hear me?"

> *Driver:* "I don't know, you must be very good, (Handle)."

> *Prostitute:* "Well, you tell me where you're at. I'll come talk to you. If all you drivers just pull in this rest area at the 150 mile marker, you can see what good booger I got for you tonight."

> *Prostitute:* "What's happening out in Buddy Park?"

> *Driver:* "Oh, there ain't much goin' on there. Ah, how you be doin'?"

> *Prostitute:* "I be doin' fine."

> *Driver:* "I be sittin' down in the rest stop, if you ain't got nothin' to do."

> *Prostitute:* "Come again?"

> *Driver:* "I'm sittin' down at the rest area, if you ain't got nothin'' to do."

> *Prostitute:* "What truck are you in?"

> *Driver:* "Look for the green trailer."

> *Prostitute:* "I hope it's not a waste of my time."

In classifying CB radio prostitution relative to other forms of prostitution, we find the effects of displacement from streets to highways (and the sophistication of the CB medium) to be evident. We are able to refer to other studies of prostitution which suggest several criteria be used in classifying the various kinds of prostitution. Karen Rosenblum (1975) suggests that three criteria can distinguish prostitutes within the hierarchy of professional status: (a) income, (b) general method of operation, and (c) clientele. Marshall Bryant (1977) provides two additional criteria: (a) appearance and (b) special talents. Charles Winick and Paul Kinsie (1971) suggest two other criteria: (a) degree of public visibility and (b) personal satisfactions afforded by the different locales of their work. Using the above criteria, we have been able to present the following profile of the CB radio prostitute (Klein and Ingle 1980b; 1981):

Income

Although prostitutes refuse to mention price over the CB radio, truckers do cite prices. The amounts we overheard (and questioned our informants about) ranged from $20.00 to $30.00 depending upon the specific service. Surprisingly, these fees remained the same over the several years (1979-1982) of our observations.

GENERAL METHOD OF OPERATION

Prostitutes and pimps arrived at Good Buddy Park and at the truck stops in their own cars equipped with a CB radio. "Pimpmobiles" (conspicuous, ostentacious cars) were seen at Good Buddy Park on a limited basis, but were not seen at the truck stops. Trucks are either already parked in the rest area and truck stops, or are passing by within CB radio range. Either a driver will call into the CB for a prostitute or a prostitute will call for a trucker. Initial calls are always on channel 19 (the trucker's channel). However, often one party will tell the other to go to a specified other channel to continue the negotiation. Through the CB, each party to the transaction will pinpoint the other's exact location. Depending upon the degree of police surveillance on any particular evening, descriptions of what each party is driving may or may not be offered. Generally, the prostitute will not offer a description of her vehicle, but will request the truck's description. ("4-wheelers," auto drivers, are not serviced.) Signalling with headlights is often a final confirmation of the trucker's vehicle, at which time the prostitute will confirm that she has spotted the correct truck and is on her way. At the cabside, further negotiation takes place. Occasionally, prostitutes can be observed not entering the truck. For one reason or another, the negotiating can be terminated at that point. However, if all goes well, the prostitute enters the cab, which usually contains a "sleeper" (cot), and remains there for ten to fifteen minutes.

Clientele

"Eighteen wheelers" (long-distance hauling truckers) are the primary target of the CB prostitute. These clientele represent, in one sense, a homogeneous group whose occupational loneliness, boredom, and isolation from sexual companionship intensify preoccupation with sexual desires.

Appearance

Our observations of appearance include the mug shots and biographical data sheets shown to us by the director of security for the three truck stops. The majority of the CB prostitutes at the locations available to us were young (teenage through their 20s) and attractive. Outfits worn by CB prostitutes are suited to the weather and are not seductive or ostentacious. The rest area and truck stop parking lots were too dimly lit for clothing to be noticed.

Special Talents

The most essential talent of the CB prostitute appears to be her ability to communicate her message over the air. Choice of "handle" (name) and language can either "turn on" or "put off" the customer.

Degree of Public Visibility

Winick and Kinsie's (1971) categories of "flagrant" and "semi-flagrant" are fitting for the bold, harsh language used over the air by CB prostitutes. Language is explicit over the air. When police surveillance is heavy, we have noticed more caution exercised. However, for the most part, the degree of public visibility (to anyone with a CB radio within listening range) is high.

Personal Satisfaction of Work Locale

Because we did not interview prostitutes, we cannot relate any direct expressions of personal satisfactions of the work locale. However, we are able to conclude from our observations that there appear to be advantages to CB talking over those of street walking. Usually, there are no gawkers or sightseers at the rest areas or truck stop parking lots. The clientele do not appear to be very selective—in fact, they usually base their entrance into the negotiation without seeing the other party. Although some drivers verbally harass and ridicule prostitutes over the CB, this is usually minimal and is probably a lot easier than taking such abuse in a face-to-face situation (as is the case for streetwalkers).

CB Pimping[2]

There is a limited amount of literature on the subject of pimping (with the exception of Ben L. Reitman's book, *The Second Oldest Profession—The Study of the Prostitute's Business Manager).* One has to search through the prostitution literature for specific references to pimping roles. We have performed such a search, which seems to yield twenty-two separate (and sometimes overlapping) roles performed by traditional pimps.

Reitman (1931) depicts the pimp as the prostitute's (1) protector against the police, (2) employment agent, (3) guard and bouncer, (4) impresario, and (5) "her man." Travis Hirschi (1962) refers to the pimp's relationship to the prostitute as a (1) "traditional" one similar to the husband-wife relationship, with the economic roles reversed. Another role of the pimp referred to by Hirschi is that of (2) a protector. According to Hirschi, a prostitute will stay within hearing range of her pimp (or friends) in order to protect herself from a violent customer. A third function of the pimp, identified by Hirschi, is that of (3) a provider of drugs. According to Hirschi (who cites several confirming sources), the pimp seduces young girls into the business and gives them drugs to keep them there. Walter Reckless (1969) refers to the (1) "procuring pimping-pandering complex." Reckless further observes that the pimp's role seems to represent a survival of a "lingering" pattern of family life—specifically (2) a patriarchal figure. Reckless notes, however, that the patriarchal role is perverted and exploitive. James H. Bryan's (1965) study of call-girl prostitution emphasizes the pimp as

(1) a contact, e.g., someone to line up clients. Bryan also found that the relationship between pimp and prostitute is "typically" one of (2) lover, although occasionally a "strictly business" relationship will exist. Further Bryan found that, among call girls, the pimp will sometimes (3) undertake the training of the girl himself, or, more typically, retain control of the training while it is conducted by another prostitute. Training, as such, is for the purpose of building up a clientele or developing a "book" of clients. Following the development of clientele, the next most important function of the pimp, according to Bryan, appears to be (4) a managerial one. Barbara Sherman Heyl (1977), in her study of House prostitution, describes the pimp's role as that of (1) recruiter and (2) connection. Heyl conducted an in-depth study of a House which specialized in training "turn-outs." From her data, it is clear that pimps are active recruiters of prostitutes. They also serve as a liaison between the newcomer and the training Madam. The "turn-outs" in Heyl's study were giving a percentage of their earnings to a pimp for a specified length of time as payment for the pimp's having placed the "turn-out" with the Madam. It should also be pointed out that 80% of the "turn-outs" coming to the Madam (in Heyl's study) did not have a long-term commitment to a pimp. Thus, the pimp's role in House prostitution is to recruit novices and place them with the Madam-trainer. (Since Madam-trainers are rare, placement with a prostitute-trainer is made instead.) In this sense, the pimp is a "connection" between the untrained (and, therefore, unmarketable) newcomer, and the potential employer, or at least the women who will give the newcomer "credentials" or experience to assist her in getting hired by another House Madam.

The content of the apprenticeship for the House prostitute seems appropriately accomplished by a Madam or other prostitute, rather than a pimp. The pimp as "coach" was not specifically found in Heyl's study (although the coaching role of pimp exists in other settings). In Heyl's study, the Madam was the coach, e.g., the one to help take the novice from "square" to "racket" values and lifestyle. It must be remembered, however, that the availability of a Madam-trainer for House prostitutes is *not* a given. Therefore, in the absence of a Madam-trainer, the newcomer may very well have to take all or a good part of her direction from her pimp.

In Heyl's study, the Madam-trainer taught techniques for (a) stimulation of the client, (b) self-defense, (c) examining a client for VD, (d) verbally manipulating the client into more expensive services ("hustling" the client), and (e) acquiring a set of occupational rules and values. Items (d) and (e) would, no doubt, be stressed by the pimp as (3) supervisor of coaching. However, it would seem likely that while the pimp may demand that the prostitute "hustle" and while he may reinforce hustling by reprisals, he may not be able to instruct as well on the specifics of accomplishing the "hustle."

Benjamin C. Carmichael (1975), depicts (1) "street hustlers" as those who provide scarce or illicit goods and services to customers. According to Carmichael, street hustlers engage in one or more of four categories of crimes, listed in rank order of desirability (e.g., income, coolness, and risk of arrest): (a) procurement-solicitation (prostitution); (b) gambling (cards, dice and pool); (c) purveying (selling drugs and stolen merchandise); and (d) general offenses (burglary, robbery, theft, etc.).

According to Carmichael, "the pimp is the most flamboyant type of street hustler and serves as the success prototype for most hustlers" (Carmichael, 1975, 145). In a validation of a popular stereotype, Carmichael notes:

> successful hustlers are flamboyant in both dress and means of transit. They dress to impress other hustlers and drive stately new automobiles, usually Cadillacs equipped with telephones, television, a bar, and small "gangster windows" in the rear. (Carmichael, 1975, 141)

With regard to the relationship between pimp and prostitute, Carmichael finds that prostitutes work "out of devotion" to a pimp and that the pimp "is keenly aware of his responsibilities to treat his women in a way that will continually elicit their devotion" (Carmichael, 1975, 146). Thus, to Carmichael, the pimp is (2) an object of devotion. Carmichael identifies three additional roles of pimps: (3) a protector, (4) companion, and (5) legal liaison. These three functions are summarized by Carmichael in the following:

> After "giving game" to his prostitutes about soliciting customers and establishing rapport with and among them, little else is required of a pimp except providing immediate and assured protection and occasional companionship. . .when arrested, a prostitute calls her pimp or bail bondsman or a "prostitute attorney," one retained ad hoc by her pimp. (Carmichael, 1975, 145)

The preceding twenty-two pimping roles may be summarized as follows:

Reitman:	(1)	protector against police
	(2)	employment agent
	(3)	guard-bouncer
	(4)	impresario
	(5)	"her man"
Hirschi:	(6)	husband (with economic role reversed)
	(7)	protector against violent customers
	(8)	provider (purveyor) of drugs
Reckless:	(9)	procurer/panderer
	(10)	patriarch (perverted and exploitive)
Bryan:	(11)	contact
	(12)	lover
	(13)	supervisor of training
	(14)	manager
Heyl:	(15)	recruiter
	(16)	connection for training
	(17)	supervisor of coaching
Carmichael:	(18)	"hustler"
	(19)	object of devotion
	(20)	protector
	(21)	companion
	(22)	legal liaison

We shall list here the order of priority that any of the aforementioned roles have in CB prostitution, thereby indicating which ones do not seem to apply to CB prostitution. We shall use our "informant pimp and prostitute"—"Ornery" and "Touché" as illustrative (although CB dialogue and systematic observation confirm much of what Ornery and Touché told us).[3]

1. Protector. The role of protector is probably the single most important role of Ornery (and other pimps observed by us). Ornery brings and parks his car close to the customer's truck and lets Touché out to enter into the truck within his view. Touché switches the trucker's CB radio channel to one mutually agreed upon by her and Ornery, so that Ornery may listen for any possible distress call from Touché. (Distress could be due to an unruly customer, an undercover police officer posing as a trucker, or a security guard interrupting the transaction.)

2a. Business manager (employment agent). Touché turns over all her money to Ornery. They live together as "man and wife." While Ornery claims to earn $400,000 per year from drug dealing and prostitution (one girl only), he has saved no money. His plan is to save and pimp for about two more years. From our observations, it appears that a "business manager" is not as functionally important to the girl as it is more of a justification for remuneration for the services that the pimp provides, e.g., protection, etc.

2b. Lover-companion-patriarch. Ornery calls Touché his wife, although it appeared to us that she is his common-law wife. They are a monogamous couple (if one does not include Touché's customers). Ornery did have other girls working with Touché, but he discontinued the others because of outbreaks of what he calls "feminine jealousy." We recognize that while the "couple-like" relationship is important to Ornery and Touché, if a pimp has several girls working for him (as we have observed), it becomes complicated to maintain a monogamous relationship.

3a. Coach-trainer-tutor. Ornery takes credit for perfecting Touché's style, e.g., how to talk on the radio, how to switch channels (to "throw off" police), how to hide her earnings from police (Touché has a slit cut in her jeans inside the area where the belt goes. She rolls up the driver's money and slides it into the hiding place until she rejoins Ornery to give it to him.)

3b. Legal liaison. Ornery and Touché have been arrested several times at the three OKC truck stops. We observed Touché's mug shot and "bio" in the "booking room" of one of the truck stops. A truck stop manager and the director of security indicated to us that Touché and Ornery were well-known to the security guards who have arrested them. When Ornery is not arrested with Touché, he posts bond for her. When he is also arrested, he calls a friend. The penalty for trespassing on the truck stop property is a $35 fine. For soliciting within OKC limits, the fine is $300. After bond is posted, Touché and Ornery do not appear on their court date and, instead, forfeit bond (which is the amount of the fine). No complex legal needs appear to exist.

4a. "Hustling." Ornery "hustles" as a purveyor of drugs (but not as a "purveyor" of girls to the customer). Ornery is not flamboyant. In fact, Ornery's "pimpmobile" is an 8-year old Oldsmobile wagon. His CB radio is from Montgomery Wards. At the cite of our earlier observations (Good Buddy Park), we observed an occasional flamboyantly dressed pimp with a stylish pimpmobile. However, the CB radio pimp's car is his means of pimping. To draw attention to it would defeat the clandestine method involved in CB pimping.

4b. Procurer (of drugs). Ornery "deals" drugs, mostly "speed" and marijuana. He is careful not to blatantly discuss drugs over the air. Truckers are his primary customers. Touché may occasionally discuss a sale in code over the air, but will usually wait until she can talk to Ornery in private. It should be noted that the student who befriended Ornery did so by overhearing a drug sale over the CB, and by questioning Ornery about it.

5a. Panderer. Ornery does not take credit for approaching prospective prostitutes for the purpose of "turning them out." Ornery has been pimping for three years. He is 35 years old. Touché is 21 years old and has been a prostitute for seven years. Touché and Ornery met three years ago. Ornery feels that it was a mutual decision for Touché to continue in prostitution. He does not take credit for pandering any of the girls who have worked for him in the past. We note that Ed Armstrong (1980) could not find any support in his study for pimps pandering ("approaching") young potential prostitutes in NYC's Port Authority bus terminal.

5b. Recruiter. Ornery has helped "facilitate" the entrance of several girls into CB radio prostitution, although he does not seek out new recruits. He feels that new recruits seek him out because of his reputation. Apparently, in CB prostitution, a novice needs very little more than a CB radio to begin making her contacts with customers. In our earlier observations of Good Buddy Park, we found that the majority of girls at that site were "outlaw prostitutes"—those who work independently (without a pimp).

In order of priority, the above five roles stand out as most important in CB pimping, and, in particular, appear to have relevance to Ornery. Although the traditional role of "ancillary crimes" does not appear to be part of Ornery's repertoire, we did observe evidence of this role by other CB pimps at Good Buddy Park. Ornery denies any purposeful involvement in any ancillary crimes other than drug dealing. It should be noted that at one truck stop, the manager had been sniped at on his way home from work. The manager is a "trouble shooter" for the oil company which owns the truck stop. He was sent to Oklahoma specifically to "clean up" the truck stop of prostitution and the accompanying drug dealing. He has been very successful at curtailing prostitution, but believes that his life and those of his family are in jeopardy, as he has received threats. (This particular truck stop manager eventually did receive a transfer to another state.) Ornery denies any specific involvement in an attempted shooting of this truck stop manager. Ornery does admit to having been involved in an occasional fight at the truck stops, usually with an unruly customer. According to Ornery, there are no "Murphy games" or other "con games" going on at the sites at which he works. From our observations of Good Buddy Park, there have been several shootings, knifings, assaults, and cars set on fire, which were believed to have been perpetrated by pimps. These incidents were confirmed by the local authorities, although no suspects were apprehended.

CONCLUSION

Our description of CB prostitution and pimping is limited to a case study of four locations in Oklahoma. Through our unobtrusive observations and eavesdropping (supplemented by informant interviews), we are able to characterize the style of CB prostitution (and pimping). Unfortunately, we lack the necessary data to characterize the role of police strategy in this type of prostitution. We have tape-recorded CB radio conversations between police and prostitutes, demonstrating futile ploys on the part of police to apprehend prostitutes at Good Buddy Park. Private security (off duty police officers) are quite successful in controlling CB prostitution on private property (truck stops).

The CB prostitute shares commonalities with other types of prostitutes and has some degree of uniqueness to her method. Specifically, she entices truckers over the CB airwaves through her ability to communicate her desirability. Her clients (truckers) represent an occupational group who find it advantageous to seek impersonal, commercial sex through rest area/truck stop settings, rather than in another manner while en route.

CB pimps also share some commonalities with traditional pimps, but have no actual unique service to perform. The CB pimp appears to provide the roles of protector, legal liaison, and procurer of drugs, as well as several other minor roles.

Because CB prostitution at interstate highway rest areas presents a special problem to law enforcement, it is likely that we will see more investigation of this type of activity taking place by those interested in controlling it. In our case study, when the attempts to control CB prostitution at one rest area failed, the authorities closed the rest area. Other "solutions" to this activity need to be explored. Our study attempts to introduce the reader to this relatively undocumented form of prostitution, in the hopes that further interest will be stimulated. As we learn more about CB prostitution, we can explore the alternatives for its social control.

NOTES

1. Personal communication with Don Green, Chairperson, Department of History, Central State University, Edmond, Oklahoma. It should be noted that while references to "wagon yards" are made in history texts, according to Dr. Green, it is rare and almost impossible to find "wagon-yard whores" mentioned in these same texts. Dr. Green, however, confirms that historians are aware of accounts of wagon yard prostitution.
2. Portions of our discussion of CB pimping are from Joan Luxenburg and Lloyd Klein, "Pedaling Peddlers: Pimping Through CB Radio," paper presented to the 31st meeting of the Society for the Study of Social Problems, August 1981, Toronto, Canada.

REFERENCES

Armstrong, E. (1980). Pimps as panderers. Paper presented to the 30th meeting of the Society for the Study of Social Problems. New York City, N.Y., 26 August.
Bryan, J.H. (1965). Apprenticeships in prostitution. *Social Problems, 12* (Winter), 287-297.
Bryant, M.A. (1977). Prostitution and the criminal justice system. *Journal of Police Science and Administration 5*(4), 379-389.
Carmichael, B.C. (1975). "Youth crime in urban communities: A descriptive analysis of street hustlers and their crimes. *Crime and Delinquency,* (April), 139-148.
Corzine, J. and Kirby, R. (1979) Crusing the truckers: Sexual encounters in a highway rest area. In D.H. Kelly (ed.), *Deviant Behavior,* pp. 574-591. New York: St. Martin's Press. (Reprinted from *Urban Life, 6*(2), July 1977.)
Heyl, B.S. (1977). The Madam as teacher: The training of house prostitutes. *Socal Problems, 24*(5), 545-555.
Hirschi, T. (1962). "The professional prostitute. *Berkeley Journal of Sociology, 7*(1), 33-49.
Horton, P.B. and Hunt, C.L. (1976). *Sociology,* 4th edition. New York: McGraw-Hill.
Ingle, J.L. (1980). *The streetwalker turned CB talker.* Paper presented to the 30th meeting of the Society for the Study of Social Problems. New York City, N.Y., 26 August.
Klein, L. and Ingle, J.L. (1980a). *Truckers and the art of sexual solicitation: Citizens' band radio conversation as ongoing accomplishment.* Paper presented to the 5th International Institute for Ethnomethodology and Conversational Analysis. Boston, MA, 23 August.
_____. (1980b). *Those CB hookers are giving prostitution a bad name!* Paper presented to the annual meeting of the Association for Humanist Sociology. Louisville, KY, 9 October.
_____. (1981). Sex solicitation by short wave radio. *Free Inquiry in Creative Sociology, 9*(1), 61-68.

Luxenburg, J. and Klein, L. (1981). *Pedaling peddlers: Pimping through CB radio.* Paper presented to the 31st meeting of the Society for the Study of Social Problems. Toronto, Canada, 24 August.

Reckless, W. (1969). *Vice in Chicago.* Montclair, New Jersey: Patterson, Smith.

Reitman, B.L. (1931). *The second oldest profession—The study of the prostitute's business manager.* New York: Vanguard Press.

Rosenblum, K. (1975). Female Deviance and the Female Sex Role: A preliminary investigation. *British Journal of Sociology, 26*(2), 169-184.

Troiden, R.R. (1974). Homosexual encounters in a highway rest stop. In E. Goode and R.R. Troiden (eds), *Sexual Deviance and Sexual Deviants,* pp. 211-228. New York: William Morrow.

Winick, C. and Kinsie P. (1971). *The lively commerce.* Chicago: Quadrangle.

Zeh, J. (1975). Muther truckers! *The Advocate, 172,* September 10, 24-26.

A Comparison of Delinquent Prostitutes and Delinquent Non-Prostitutes on Self-Concept

Daria S. Bour
Jeanne P. Young
Rodney Henningsen

The basic theme around which this study was organized was, "What, if any, differences could be found between delinquent groups; one prostitute and one non-prostitute?" The purpose of this study was to learn more about the ways in which delinquent prostitutes and delinquent non-prostitutes differ. The objectives of this study were: (1) to compare social and demographic statistics between juvenile prostitute groups, all of whom were recidivists remanded to secure detention in upstate New York and (2) to determine if there were significant differences between groups on the basis of self-concept as measured by the Tennessee Self Concept Scale. The methods used in this study were: (1) the collection of data on the social and demographic backgrounds of the respondents; (2) the collection of data as recorded on a questionnaire; (3) the utilization of the Tennessee Self Concept Scale (TSCS) in order to discriminate groups on the basis of self-concept; (4) obtaining a computer analysis on the TSCS scores; (5) the utilization of an electronic calculator and a digital computer to determine relative significance of variables pertinent to this study and to conduct chi square analyses; and (6) considering all results with a probability of .05 or less as significant.

Daria S. Bour is with Monroe County Children's Center, Rochester, NY, Jeanne P. Young and Rodney Henningsen are in the Criminal Justice Center, Sam Houston State University, Huntsville, TX.

This paper was presented on March 22-26, 1983, to the Academy of Criminal Justice Sciences, San Antonio, Texas.

89

JUVENILE PROSTITUTION

The study of juvenile prostitution has been approached as a "complex of manifestations reaching into the sexual, psychological, social, economic, legal and moral fields" (Carlebach, 1962). Using this perspective as a cornerstone, the following statements reflect the current theoretical schools of thought regarding the juvenile prostitute.

Sexual Theories

1. That manifest irregularities may exist in the sexual life of the parents. (Gibbons)
2. That traditionally defined sexual roles for women are confusing, making sexual choices for women difficult. (Davis)
3. That sexual delinquency may exist for the purposes of identification and survival. (Crowley, Anson, Brown, James)
4. That the approval of early sexual contact is often determined by race and culture.
5. That prostitutes as children experienced more sexual advances by elders, were more victimized by incest and experienced higher incidence of rape than those women who were not prostitutes. (Gray, Brown, James)
6. As a result of the conditions listed in number five, the victims' level of self-esteem may lessen the resistance to viewing themselves as a saleable commodity. (Brown, Gray)

Psychological Viewpoints

1. That the utilization of sex may be seen as an attempt to satisfy dominant wishes for security, recognition, and love.
2. That feelings or isolation and loss of identity may be seen in the prostitute. (Reid, Davis)
3. That for the sexual deviant, there is a rationalization of behavior, usually taking the form of exaggerating other values such as financial success or increased individual freedom. (Jackman)
4. Another rationalization is that of the love relationships suggested between girls and their pimps, with love being a culturally acceptable explanation for feelings and behavior unacceptable to others. (Baizerman, Vedder, Anson)

Social Correlates

1. That there may be a lack of parental affection and supervision including breakdown in all family relationships. (Gibbons, Gray, Brown, James)
2. That this lack of adequate family life may reflect a rejection of the traditional goals of marriage and the family.
3. That class and cultural orientation may make one vulnerable to sexual deviance.
4. That social and self labeling may add to the continuation of deviance, through both association and opportunity. (Erikson, Reid, Becker, Simmons, Lemert, Gagnon)
5. That the lack of interest in the various social institutions (school, sports, church) may relate to the development of behavioral patterns and self-concept.
6. That the sexual revolution and social change may cause the adolescent to view sexual deviance as acceptable. (Anson, McCaghy)
7. That association with runaway behavior, including drug usage, survival, institutionalization and delinquent association may promote the instance of prostitution. (Bracey, Brown, James, Anson)
8. That most common positive self perceptions are found among white females who are apprehended for commonly considered female crimes. (Datesman, Mannarino, Marsh)

Economics

1. That the need for financial gain is often related to situational requirement. . .that the girls' immediate living situations and financial circumstances proved to be important in the decision to prostitute. (Gray, Vedder, Anson)
2. That financial success is found after the need for love and acceptance is gained. (Baizerman, Brown, Datesman, Vedder, Anson)

Legal Aspects

1. That the legal system is set up so that it contains rather than deters the existence of prostitution. (Adams, Anson, Brown, James)

2. That prostitution is often a vehicle for other offenses such as property and personal crimes.
3. That the punishment for such offenses; incarceration, may act as a breeding ground and educational forum for future sexual deviants. (Adams, Kay, Gray, Brown)
4. That though the prostitute may behave in an illegitimate manner, ties to conventional behaviors continue to exist—they are just rendered ineffective in practice. (Sykes-Matza, Gagnon, Rathus, Siegel)

DEMOGRAPHIC CHARACTERISTICS

The demographic data elicited from individual folders has been appraised as follows: of the 50 respondents in the sample, 25 were prostitutes and 25 were non-prostitutes. This status was derived through self verification and from the research questionnaire. All were, at the time of testing, detained at an upstate New York secure detention facility as remanded by various family courts of New York State. Ages of both groups ranged from 13 to 15 years, the average being 14.4 years. Of the prostitute group, 9 were of white ethnic origin and 16 of black ethnic origin. For the non-prostitute group, 12 were white and 13 black.

All respondents were female and recidivists or repeat offenders. The average education level was grade 7 for both groups. This level fell at approximately 1.4 years behind the expected levels for the respective groups.

The remainder of the demographic data included possible variables elicited from the folders and research questionnaire which were thought to possibly discriminate between the two groups. These were I.Q., Psychological Diagnosis, Parental Absence, Physical and Sexual Abuse, Importance of Trustworthiness, Personal Aspirations, Self-Happiness, Religious Affiliation, Drug and Alcohol Use, School Attendance, and Sexual Experience. The research questionnaire was composed of five additional questions posed to the prostitute group only in an attempt to attain some additional information regarding the prostitute lifestyle. This accomplished, the respondents completed the Tennessee Self Concept Scale and were compared on several variables included in the test. In addition, some of the variables discussed in the demographic were again compared on the basis of self concept.

From the demographic data the research questionnaire, the variables of significant status were: *Drug Usage* and *Sexual Experience.* *Drug Usage,* on the basis of use more than twice a week, indicated that more non-prostitutes than prostitutes admitted to using drugs regularly while on the street (Table 1). Thirteen of 52% of the non-prostitute group answered in the affirmative to drug usage as compared to 6 or 24% of the prostitute group. The responses thereby suggest that prostitution incidence was not a result of drug use or addiction. However, since this assumption is at variance with some existing hypotheses, further study might be indicated and could include questioning whether or not drugs were an issue in initiating a prostitute career or at any time during the initiation process.

Sexual Experience, or particularly the age of intercourse, was the last of the demographic data to project significant group difference at the .05 level through chi square testing.

The prostitute group 20 or 80% as having had intercourse at young ages (13 or under) as compared to 16 or 64% of the non-prostitute group (Table 2). The figures present possible relationships between age of intercourse and instance of prostitution.

Other demographic variables, though not significant by means of chi square testing and analysis, may be worthy of mention and could well be areas in which further concentration is needed in the study of juvenile prostitution. The first is *Parental Absence* which was reflective of residence of the respondents. Here the prostitute group recorded 16 or 64% as living with mother only, 6 or 24% with both parents (or figures of both) and 3 or 12% with "other." From these

TABLE 1

Drug Use

Sexual Behavior			Drug Use
	Yes	No	Total
Prostitute	6(24%)	19(76%)	25
Non-Prostitute	13(52%)	12(48%)	25
Total	19(38%)	31(62%)	50

P < .05   df = 1 x^2 = 4.158

TABLE 2

Sexual Experience

Sexual Behavior   Age of First Sexual Intercourse

	13 or under	14 or 15	Never	Total
Prostitute	20(80%)	5(20%)	0	25
Non-Prostitute	16(64%)	3(12%)	6(24%)	25
Total	36(72%)	8(16%)	6(12%)	25

$$P < .05 \quad df = 2 \quad x^2 = 6.944$$

figures, the suggestion is that more of the prostitute group reported living with mother only and more of the non-prostitute group reported residence with both parents.

Personal Aspirations was another variable which indicated some discrepancy between the groups. Finishing School appeared to be of greater importance to the non-prostitute group in that 10 or 40% of the non-prostitute group reported "yes" to this as compared with 6 or 24% of the prostitute. Continuing, *School Attendance* reflects similar response, with the prostitute group 12 or 48% of whom not attending was twice that of the non-prostitute group in the same category, 6 or 24% of whom were not attending. Also found under *Personal Aspirations,* the replies to the question of getting married were interesting. In this case, more non-prostitutes, 10 or 40%, than prostitutes, 3 or 12% seemed quite intent on *not* getting married. The figures for this sample ran against some current hypothetical belief that prostitutes might be more inclined not to desire the marital role, in that they, more frequently than non-prostitutes, may have been exposed to faulty family relationships. Whether or not such a hypothesis has statistical importance requires further study with consideration for the issues of fantasizing and/or exaggerating emphasis placed on certain familial roles.

The five additional questions posed to the prostitute group are summarized as follows: The first question, "Is this your main source of income" elicited negative responses from all 25 tested. Income sources were posited as relatives, legitimate odd jobs and boyfriends. None of the girls claimed to be self-supporting. All reported residence with some type of family orientation.

The second question, "Who first introduced you to this way of earning money," elicited several responses. Eleven, and the majority of the respondents, listed "Boyfriend." "Friends" comprised 7 more. The last response "other" included sisters, uncles and brother.

Given these replies, it is suggested that one does not make the decision to prostitute alone, rather, one is introduced to it, becoming involved through association, opportunity structures or alignment with other labeled deviants (Becker, 1963).

The third question, "Where are your contacts made," was answered in three categories and included "night clubs," "street" and "local restaurants." The girls explained that the three usually are combined in some manner; that location depends on public need, weather and direction of "bosses" or "pimps." The issue of legal drinking age was not an issue here as there appeared to be no problem in falsifying identification to accommodate entrance into drinking establishments.

Question four, "What are the benefits to earning money in this manner," elicited the possible "why" to the issue of juvenile prostitution. Of the responses, financial reward and personal attention and affection were obvious in the majority of replies.

The final question, "How long do you think your career might last," drew three standard answers. The first and most prominent included the intention of marrying (usually the pimp) and starting a family. The second revolved around obtaining legitimate jobs. The third response, which included 7 of the prostitute sample, suggested that they might continue to prostitute "as the need arises." it was in this category that they felt that prostitution was a security to fall back on and to be used as a matter of circumstance.

Off the record questions were asked about pimps but disclosures was found difficult to obtain. None of the girls appeared to be eager about this discussion.

The Tennessee Self Concept Scale was the final discriminator for the groups and this scale was also used to analyze the groups on certain of the demographic variables.

Only one variable from the TSCS proved to be statistically significant and that was the item of Physical Self (Table 3). It was for this case that almost twice as many prostitutes as non-prostitutes scored above the norm. The remainder of the scores were quite comparable for both groups. Neither group showed evidence of psychotic or neurotic reaction. The sample in total did score below the norm in terms of overall self concept; the total mean for the prostitute group was 309.52 as compared to 309.64 for the non-prostitute

TABLE 3

How the Respondent Perceives the Physical Self

Group	↑Norm	↓Norm	Non-D.
Pros.	13(52%)	9(36%)	3(12%)
Non-Pros.	7(28%)	18(72%)	0

$$P< .05 \quad df = 2 \quad x^2 = 7.8$$

group. The norm score from the TSCS Manual was 345.57. Hence, not only did the groups differ significantly from each other but they were also not grossly lower than the norm mean.

CONCLUSIONS

There were three basic questions and seven hypotheses posed to guide the direction of this study and to ascertain whether the data would substantiate the hypotheses. The difference in demographic data between the groups was significant for *Drug Use* and *Age of Intercourse.* The inferences to be made from these differences are that (1) drug users are more common among non-prostitutes, and (2) juvenile prostitutes are more likely to experience sexual intercourse at an earlier age. Parental absence held promise of being a factor in distinguishing prostitutes from non-prostitutes as almost twice as many prostitutes recorded living with mother only as non-prostitutes, who recorded living with both parents or in some other familial setting. This promise did not materialize as being significant at the .05 level upon chi square testing.

With regard to self-concept, the groups were significantly different on only one scale: the *Physical Self* where the prostitute group scored above the norm almost twice as frequently as the non-prostitute group. According to contemporary labeling theorists, it makes sense that prostitutes would receive enhanced positive reactions in terms of their physical prowess given the trade and exposure.

It may be posited at this point, then, that the factors involved in developing the decision to prostitute may be early sexual intercourse and a positive view of one's physical attributes. It is difficult to conclude, however, that the attitude toward physical self is developed before or after the onset of prostitute status.

Regarding the hypotheses generated by this study, the data indicated that the first hypothesis, i.e., *that there will not be significant differences in self-concept between groups* was not fully rejected. The variable from the TSCS which proved to be statistically significant was that of *Physical Self,* in which the prostitute group fared higher than both the non-prostitute group and the norm taken from the TSCS Manual. The total self concept scores for the groups were strikingly similar and were somewhat but not significantly different from the norm mean. The bulk of the respondents felt happy with themselves on a sometimes basis. Thus, the hypothesis that the groups would not be different in terms of self concept was, for the most part, substantiated by the data.

The second hypothesis was *that there would be no significant differences in social/demographic data collected for the two groups.* This hypothesis was rejected in that there were two distinct and significant differences between the groups. The first, *Drug Usage,* showed a higher use level within the non-prostitute group. The second group differentiator, *Age of Intercourse,* appeared to be the most intriguing in terms of suggesting possible rationale for entering prostitution, as the prostitute group had experienced intercourse at an earlier age than the non-prostitute group. Interestingly, *Age of Intercourse* did not appear to be a significant factor in discriminating groups on the basis of self concept as might have been expected.

The third hypothesis stated *that parental abuse, physical or sexual, would not be a factor in the decision to prostitute.* This hypothesis was substantiated in full, as the groups did not differ demographically or in terms of the self concept regarding these variables.

The fourth hypothesis stated *that parental absence was not of major importance in the decision to prostitute.* This hypothesis was accepted as no significance was found in discriminating between groups, either in the demographic data or in comparison on the basis of self concept.

The fifth hypothesis posited *that age of intercourse would not be a factor in the discrimination between the groups.* This hypothesis was rejected in that the prostitute group had experienced intercourse at an earlier age than the non-prostitute group. Hence, age of intercourse appears to be reliable factor in the decision to prostitute. Still, age of intercourse did not differentiate in terms of self concept so that the theoretical assumption that low self concept might be a result of one's sexual predicament is rejected. This rejection is verified in that self concept was not a factor related to *Physical* and *Sex-*

ual Abuse, as the groups were not significantly differentiated on these bases.

The sixth hypothesis stated *that I.Q. levels would not reveal significant differences between the two groups.* This hypothesis is supported on the basis that no significant differences in I.Q. were found between the groups, either as related to demographics or to self concept as measured by the TSCS.

The final hypothesis posited *that the majority of both groups would aspire to conventional lifestyles and believe that their ability to achieve such is possible.* The analysis of this hypothesis was gauged by the responses to questions regarding *Personal Aspirations* and included such items as finishing school, getting married and having children. Assuming that these variables are akin to "conventional" aspirations, the groups did, as a whole, respond favorably to all three items and the hypothesis is accepted. In addition, the prostitute group appeared to quite favorably be intent on assuming the roles of wife/mother. This finding was contrary to the suggestion in the review of the literature that prostitutes might reject such ideals in that they had not been exposed to earlier successful family relationships. Again, the possibility is not ruled out, however, that these aspirations were related to fantasizing.

RECOMMENDATIONS

It is hoped that this study will generate areas of interest to others who may be involved in the study of juvenile delinquency and prostitution. Among such areas might be: (1) further study on the aspect of parental absence and its effects on juvenile prostitution; (2) an in-depth look at the variables of physical and sexual abuse and its impact on juvenile prostitution; (3) why prostitutes appear to score higher on the *Physical Self* appraisal on the TSCS than non-prostitutes; (4) continued exploration on the role of the pimp in juvenile prostitution; (5) enhanced discussion on the legal and moral responsibilities regarding juvenile prostitution; (6) further study involving the utilization of drugs as an initiating factor or at any time during the process of becoming a prostitute; and (7) consideration for possible fantasy aspirations or exaggerated emphasis placed on the roles of marriage, wifehood, and motherhood, particularly by juvenile prostitutes.

PROGRAM RECOMMENDATIONS

Thus far, the program recommendations developed in an attempt to eradicate the problem of juvenile prostitution can be categorized as being legal and social. From the legal perspective, Hanna (1979) has offered a variety of techniques to be possibly used in dealing with the prostitution problem:

1. Utilization of suggestions of men assigned to the problem.
2. That patrol people and investigators must work together.
3. The utilization of reserves, citizens, and disguises while working decoys.
4. Developing knowledge on the techniques of the local prosecutor.
5. Convincing the judges of the seriousness of the problem.
6. Male decoy cases.
7. Female decoy cases.
8. Observation cases.
9. Issuance of county health department examination appointments.
10. Working with hotels and motels.
11. The issuance of traffic citations.
12. The making of warrant checks on known prostitutes and pimps.
13. Filing prior convictions to obtain mandatory 45 and 90 day sentences.
14. Enforcement of probation conditions.
15. Additional penal code sections.
16. Red light district abatement laws.
17. Massage parlor ordinances.

The above suggestions are to be carried out on a consistent and uniform basis. It is Hanna's feeling that strict legal discipline may dissuade the would-be prostitutes from making that first decision.

The social perspective has dealt with societal remedies. Srivastava (1982) suggests that repressive measures have failed miserably in solving the prostitution problem. A strategy is needed that is more pragmatic and less moralistic. He looks at the obstacles to rehabilitation and suggests that rehabilitation efforts be focused on women and girls who have been forced into prostitution and want to get out. For those, much must be done to provide them with education and vocational skills, guidance and a healthy home. Further, repression should be directed at those who profit from the women. Along these same lines, Gray (1973) states that thus far the punishment has been mild and infrequently administered, which appears to have been ineffective as a deterrent. Gray posits that two elements may break the cycle: "(1) The formation of a close, intimate attachment to a conventional person who strongly disapproves of her involvement; or (2) the removal of the opportunity for her to engage in prostitution" (p. 423). In agreement with Gray, James (1979) offers two more recommendations: "First, remedial education in public schools and correctional facilities must address the largely negative, punitive effect of prior academic experience. Second, strong, positive role models are needed from which a new value system may develop. The importance of the absence of "significant others," (from conforming members of the community), in the girls' lives cannot be overstated, and without it, the failure to adopt mainsteam values remains (p. 677).

The public has yet to, and may never see, whether or not such programs will have any impact as to the problem of juvenile prostitution. In answer to this, documentation and analysis of new and existing programs is necessitated.

BIBLIOGRAPHY

Anson, R. S., Bodies for Sale: End of the Road for Runaways. *Mademoiselle,* August, 1981.
Baizerman, M. Thompson, J. Stafford-White, K. An old, young friend. Adolescent prostitution. *Children Today, 8*(5), Sept.-Oct., 1979.
Brown, M. Teenage prostitution. *Adolescence, XLV*(56), Winter, 1979.
Carlebach, J. (Child Welfare Society of Kenya) Juvenile prostitutes in Nairobi. Applied Research Unit, East African Institute of Social Research, Kampala, Uganda, 1962.
Crowley, M. G. *Female runaway behavior and its relationship to prostitution.* Thesis, Sam Houston State University, May, 1977.
Davis, K. The sociology of prostitution. *American Sociological Review, 2,* 1937.
Gagnon, J. H. *Human sexuality.* Glenville, Illinois: Scott, Foresman and Co.
Gibbons, D. C. *Delinquent behavior.* Englewood Cliffs, New Jersey: Prentice-Hall, Inc.
———. Society, crime and criminal careers. Englewood Cliffs, New Jersey: Prentice-Hall, Inc.
Gray, D. Turning out: A study of teenage prostitution. *Urban Life and Culture, 1*(4), January, 1973.
Hanna, R. E. Combating prostitution: Salinas police curb city's street problem. Salinas P.D., Salinas, California, *Police Chief,* 1979.
Jackman, N. R., O'Toole, R., Geis, G. The self-image of the prostitute. *Sociological Quarterly, 4,* Spring, 1963.
James, J., Meyerding, J. Early sexual experience and prostitution. *American Journal of Psychiatry, 134*(12), December, 1977.

James, J. Motivations for entrace into prostitution. *The Female Offender,* (Laura Crites, editor). Lexington, Massachusetts: Heath and Co.; Washington D.C.: Lexington Books, 1976.

James, J. *Prostitution and addiction: An interdisciplinary approach.* Seattle: University of Washington, 1977.

James, J. Teenage prostitutes. *Adolescence, XIV*(56), Winter, 1979.

Mannarino, A. Marsh, M. E. The relationship between sex role identification and juvenile delinquency in adolescent girls. *Adolescence, XIII*(52), Winter, 1978.

McCaghy, C. H., *Deviant behavior, crime, conflict and interest groups.* New York, Macmillan Publishing Co., Inc., 1976.

Reid, S. T. *Crime and criminology.* Hinsdale, Illinois: The Dryden Press, 1976.

Simmons, J. L. *Deviants.* Berkeley, California: The Glendessary Press, 1969.

Srivostava, S. P. Rehabilitation of fallen women and girls—Need for a new outlook. Dept. of Social Work, Luckinow U., *Indian Journal of Criminology, 101,* 1982.

Sykes, G., Matza, D. Techniques of neutralization: A theory of delinquency. In Marvin E. Wolfgang et al., eds., *The sociology of crime and delinquency,* 2nd edition. New York: Wiley, 1970.

Vedder, C. B., Somerville, D. B. *The delinquent girl.* Springfield, Illinois: Charles C. Thomas, Publisher, 1973.

An Analysis of the Factors Related to the Rate of Violent Crimes Committed by Incarcerated Female Delinquents

Mary L. Balthazar
Ruall J. Cook

Juvenile delinquency has been a subject creating much social concern. It occurs in every community, affecting children of all religious beliefs and socioeconomic class, and every ethnic group. In the state of Louisiana, thousands of juveniles are arrested and incarcerated each year for committing a crime.

Present concern about juvenile delinquency is but a continuation of parental and public anxiety beginning before written records. Many of the actual types of delinquency are the same now as thousands of years ago. Undoubtedly, the most disturbing fact of this recidivism of delinquency and crime on the part of our young people is that no society has mastered the technique of successfully initiating all children into the expectation and demands of their society and thus avoiding the problem of delinquency. Today each society struggles with the twin problems of the socialization of its children and the rehabilitation of its deviants.

The fundamanetal purpose of this study was to show the variations, if any existed, in the rate of violent crimes among female juveniles according to age, educational level, I.Q., family structure, and geographical location. This study attempted to explain these factors and their relationship to the rate of violent crimes committed by female juveniles.

In reviewing the literature it was obvious that many authors regarded juvenile delinquency by girls not to be a significant factor in crime and delinquent behavior. The need to present a more current or up-to-date view of female juvenile delinquency is still in demand in order to provide a more pragmatic definition of juvenile delinquency, determine the direct causes of juvenile delinquency and to explore the behavior and apparent significant increase in female juvenile delinquency. This study has focused primarily on some of the factors that could possibly be significant in influencing the rate of violent crimes committed by female juveniles incarcerated in Louisiana. Such factors include age, educational level, I.Q., family structure and geographical location.

The criminality of females is a neglected field of research and it is evident that more research in this area is greatly needed. With changing sex roles and increasing involvement by females in a broad spectrum of activities, it is no wonder that recent statistics indicate an increase in the arrest rate of females (Thornburg, 1975). According to Thornburg, the increase in female delinquency probably represents (1) a percentage of girls who want to play a more masculine role and see the opportunity to do so; (2) a percentage of girls who are in a stage of conflict, caught between the stereotyped traditional role and the more active female role; and (3) a percentage of girls who simply feel unable to live up to their role expectations at home, in school, and among their peers.

The increase in violent crime by girls is in keeping with a trend toward an increase in violent crime among juveniles in general (Kratcoski & Kratcoski, 1979). Most books and research dealing with juvenile delinquency that were published before 1960 specifically focused on it as a problem of adolescent boys. If girls were mentioned in the discussion at all, they were given scant attention. However, the number of arrests of female juveniles has risen dramatically since 1960, with a corresponding narrowing of the gap between the sexes in the rates of delinquency. In 1960, the number of males arrested under age 18 was 414,082 and the number of females under age 18 arrested in the same year was 70,925, producing a 6-to-1 ratio of male to female arrests. By 1976, the arrest ratio of male-female juveniles had dropped to 3.5-to-1. There seems to have been an increased tendency for females to commit violent offenses and felonies. From 1960-1975, the number of females arrested for murder increased 275%, those arrested for robbery increased 64% and those arrested for aggravated robbery increased 438%. Offenses against property by females increased, and the number of arrests for larceny-theft by females increased 458%. The arrests for buying, receiving or possessing stolen property by females increased 824% in the same 15 year period (Kratcoski & Kratcoski, 1979).

VIOLENT CRIMES COMMITTED BY FEMALE JUVENILES

The classification of offenses is controlled up to a certain point. The crime classification does not include all the many types of minor offenses for which many female juveniles are not incarcerated. Girls who might be reprimanded by the police without formal arrest are not included in data obtained for the Uniform Crime Reports. Not all girls who commit delinquent acts are included among the arrest or court cases. Some misbehaviors even of a serious nature are not detected by responsible adults; some are detected, but not by the police, and some are not referred to the police. The explanation for the juvenile not being referred varies case by case. For example, neighbors may adjust payment for property damage with the parents of the offending child. Storekeepers may stop a young shoplifter as she leaves the store and relieve her of stolen articles; many types of delinquent behavior occurring in and near school property are handled by school officials. Many minor delinquencies are simply passed over by observers, even by the victims, as part of the process of growing up. The delinquency that comes to the courts' attention is a combination of an immoderate amount of "normal" deviation and serious offenses which threaten or injure.

Violent crime has been categorized in five ways according to Miller (1966). His categorization includes (1) *forms of crime directed at persons,* in which distinctions were based on age, gang membership, and number of actors and targets; (2) *forms of crime directed at objects,* in which distinctions were based on mode of inflicting damage; (3) *forms of crime directed at persons and objects,* in which distinctions were based on official clasifications; (4) *targets of crime directed at persons,* in which distinctions were based on age, sex, race, gang membership, and collectivity; and (5) *targets of crime directed at objects,* in which distinctions were based on the identity of the object.

The formerly held belief that delinquency among girls is predominantly sex-related no longer squares with official statistics. It is noted that less than 1% of the total arrests of females under 18 were for specifically sex-related offenses such as prostitution, commercialized vice, or sex offenses (FBI, Uniform Crime Reports for the United States, 1977). In contrast, 33% of these arrests were for violent crime or property crime (FBI, Uniform Crime Reports for the United States, 1977).

An increased involvement of females in serious crimes has occurred in recent years. For example, females accounted for nearly 20% of all arrests for serious crimes in 1976, whereas in 1960 they made up only 11% of the total. The chief increases in crime for females as a group have occurred in property crimes. However, the trends for females under 18 years of age differ from those for females in general, showing a steady pattern of increase in arrests for violent and property crimes. Females accounted for only 7% of the violent crimes by the under-18 age group in 1960, but this had risen to 10% by 1971 and 11% by 1976. In property crime, females made up 9% of the arrests in 1960, 17% in 1971, and 19% in 1976 (FBI, Uniform Crime Reports for the United States, 1977).

Freda Adler defined a trend toward more aggressive behavior by institutionalized females at all levels of the correctional system, and predicted that before long, female inmates will behave a great deal like male inmates (Adler, 1975).

Females committed to long-term institutions for delinquents have been placed there more frequently for status offenses than for delinquent acts. For example, a comparison of boys and girls in Colorado training schools showed that most of the males incarcerated there had been involved in burglary, robbery, or car theft, whereas most of the females had been committed for incorrigibility, sex offenses, or running away (Barker and Adams, 1972).

These statistics reveal the need for more careful research involving female delinquency and the increase of violent crime.

Many studies have revealed a relationship between age, educational level, I.Q., family structure and geographical location to the rate of crimes committed by female juveniles.

Age and delinquency have a direct relationship. According to Gold, delinquency begins to rise sharply at age 12, peaks at age 15, and begins to decline thereafter (Gold, 1970). Hirschi (1969) and Hindelang (1973) both correlate greater delinquency with lower academic achievement (Johnson, 1979).

The relationship between age and delinquency is, of course, one of the central problems of criminology. The most important question relating to the age of the delinquent concerns his/her maturation, or the age at which delinquency is highest at some time during adolescence, usually between 14 and 16 and falls away rapidly after 21, or at most, 25. The majority of children or adolescents who appear before a court do so only once; and the majority of those who persist for a time stop their criminal behavior, or at least are not arrested, after the age of 21, or at most, 25. On the whole, the younger the delinquent at first conviction, the greater the chances of reconviction. Sheldon and Eleanor Glueck, from a study of their massive data, reached a somewhat intermediate conclusion that delinquency "regardless of age at the time it begins. . .runs a fairly steady and predictable course" (Glueck and Glueck, 1940), "on the whole, if the acts of delinquency begin very early in life, they are abandoned at a relatively early stage of adulthood, provided various mental abnormalities do not counteract the natural tendency to maturation. . . .If, on the other hand, the acts of delinquency begin in adolescence, the delinquent tendency seems to run its course into a later stage of adulthood, again, however, provided the natural process of maturation is not interfered with" (Glueck and Glueck, 1945).

In European countries, the age of criminal responsibility varies widely from 8 or 10 to 14, 15, or 16; it does not necessarily follow that the treatment provided differs widely.

In Germany, England, Canada, and Japan, there appears to be an increase in recorded delinquency in the older adolescent age group.

In Germany, adult crime has remained relatively constant in the last ten years; the general increase in crime is mainly attributed to an increase in juvenile crime, especially in the age groups 18-21, and to some extent in younger groups.

In Japan, adult crime has been steadily decreasing for the last six years, but crime has been held constant by an increase in the age group 15-18. By special police measures and other facilities, the crime rate in this age group has, however, been stabilized in the last two years.

Many believe that with increased mobility and industrialization, there is an increased tendency to report offenses that occur in cities. It is, however, uncertain whether certain age groups are more particularly affected by these changes.

A study conducted at the Magdalen Hospital School for intermediate and senior girls, with age range from 14 to 17, showed that as the age of 15 is approached, disturbed behavior of the delinquent type becomes more and more within the span of normal reaction, taking the emotional instability of puberty into account. At this age, there is a sharp rise in the incidence of delinquency in girls.

According to the cases handled by courts reporting to the United States Children's Bureau, the predominating interval in age distribution was that between 14 and 16 years of age, the interval between 16 and 21 being a close second in order. Both of these age intervals had more than twice the number of cases as did the next interval, namely, that between age 12 and 14. However, since there is a great variation by states in the upper and lower age limits of cases handled by courts, these interval distributions are not wholly accurate. Most states do not consider as delinquent children under certain ages, but the minimum age varies in different states; and the upper age of cases handled by juvenile courts ranges from 16 to 21 in the different states. Since in some states the juvenile courts do not have jurisdiction over a person beyond the age of 16, statistics based on cases disposed of by juvenile courts are not reliable regarding the chronological age factor in delinquency.

It is significant to note that manifestations of misbehavior may originate early in childhood, increase with age up to a certain point, and then decline. The peak age of delinquency and crime depends upon the group studied.

Some authors have found that girls seem to get started in delinquency later than do boys.

EDUCATION LEVEL AND I.Q. OF FEMALE JUVENILES

According to Hardy and Cull (1975), if a child comes from an inadequate family situation, entry into the school system will likely enhance the child's problems. A study at the Magdalen Hospital School in Southern England suggested that it was principally for the youngest children that deficiency of intelligence increases the risk of delinquency (Slater, Cowie, and Cowie, 1968). Woodward (1955) thought the best estimate of the mean intelligence of delinquents in the U.S.A. was 92 and in England not less than 90. Woodward stressed an important factor which might tend to depress the test results of delinquents. She expressed the idea that delinquents are commonly emotionally unstable, and emotional upsets may reduce the level of performance under stress. Pollak (1950) found that the intelligence factor seemed to play a very small role in the criminality of females. No significant relationship between low intelligence and criminality has ever been reliably documented by research studies (Kratcoski and Kratcoski, 1979).

Glueck and Glueck (1970) in their study of 500 juvenile offenders found that out of 478 cases studied 73% had low verbal intelligence.

FAMILY STRUCTURE OF FEMALE JUVENILES

In the family, structure is observed through interactional patterns. The members define themselves in interaction. When a mother sends a verbal or non-verbal message to a child, she is defining who she is in relation to him and who he is in relation to her. Family structure grows and expresses itself through this transactional definition of selves (Pollak and Friedman, 1969). A child has no control over the actual structure of the family: whether or not grandparents are present. The child's family composition of siblings is also not within the realm of his control (Haskell and Yablonsky, 1978).

Nye (1958) stated that the structure of the family itself does not cause delinquency. For example, the fact that a home is broken does not cause delinquency, but it is more difficult for a single parent to provide material needs, direct controls, and other important elements of family life. Children in small families have a better chance to develop very close relationships to parents, which facilitate indirect control by parents, than do those in large families.

Toby (1957) argues that the association between a broken home and delinquency is much more evident in the case of girls than boys. Toby writes: "The family not only transmits socially accepted values to the next generation, it also seeks to prevent the child from being influenced by deviant patterns. The better integrated the family, the more successful it is as a bulwark against antisocial influences emanating from the neighborhood or the peer group. However, the differences between the protection afforded by well-integrated and disorganized families is greater for girls and pre-adolescents than for adolescent boys" (Toby, 1957). Wattenberg and Saunders (1954) found a higher proportion of broken homes among female juvenile offenders.

Girls from broken homes more frequently than girls from unbroken homes, (1) drove a car without a license; (2) were truant from school; (3) ran away from home; (4) bought or drank alcohol; and (5) had heterosexual relationships.

Divorce, death, separation and desertion break and disrupt family ties. This unstable, disruptive family has often been cited as an important contribution to juvenile delinquency. Glueck and Glueck investigated the relationship between broken homes and juvenile delinquency and found over half of delinquents in their sample were raised in single-parent families, while only 10% of the non-delinquents had such a background (Griffen and Griffen, 1978).

GEOGRAPHICAL LOCATION OF FEMALE JUVENILES

In the 1930s, among the sociological studies of delinquency that sought to relate it to the influence of the urban environment were the activities of the Chicago group, researchers associated with the Chicago Area Project of the University of Chicago. Clifford Shaw and his associates divided the city of Chicago into zones and examined the number of official delinquency referrals in various parts of the city. They found the volume of delinquent activity to be greatest in the center of the city, where the neighborhoods were changing from residential to urban and where the housing was deteriorated and crowded (Shaw, 1929).

A number of more recent researchers have also sought to located the delinquency areas of large cities: a comparison of data from Indianapolis, Baltimore, and Detroit revealed that despite other dissimilarities, the cities all tended to have zones with high levels of delinquency and that these were characterized by overcrowded, substandard housing. The residents of these zones were chiefly those with low incomes and minimal occupational skills (Chilton, 1972).

The incidence of reported juvenile delinquency is significantly higher in some areas than in others. The cities have higher per capita rates than the suburbs, and the suburbs, in turn, have higher rates than rural areas (Short, 1966).

A girl growing up in a high-delinquency area has few positive adult models in the community to emulate. The high-delinquency area maximizes the temptations for illegitimate behavior and minimizes the external inhibitions. In situations like this, the young females, along with everyone else, are engaged in what is literally a battle for survival. The environment places a reward on aggressiveness, on living for the moment without worry over the past or future, and on the ability to get as much as possible or what little there is for oneself (McCandless, 1967). Such a tough, egocentric, cynical attitude is naturally conducive to delinquent behavior.

Rural female adolescents have been considered to be less delinquent for a variety of reasons: (1) more work to occupy their time, (2) more recognition for work, (3) more effective social controls, and (4) fewer social contacts. These assumptions have occasionally been contested on the grounds that behavior that would possibly be classified as delinquency in urban areas is not reported to the law enforcement personnel as such. Even behavior considered delinquent in rural areas is often handled on an informal basis and is not entered into police records.

METHODOLOGY

The dependent variable for this study was the rate of violent crimes committed by female juveniles. Violent crimes were defined as crimes committed against another person such as murder, manslaughter, homicide, assault and battery, robbery, and armed robbery. A female juvenile delinquent was defined as any female under the age of 22 who was incarcerated for committing a crime.

The independent variables were as follows:

1. *Age*—calculated in months.
2. *Educational Level*—last grade completed at the time of admission to the juvenile institution.
3. *I.Q.*—scores received on the WAIS administered by psychologist.
4. *Family Structure*—coded as one of the following: (a) father and mother; (b) mother only; (c) father only; (d) father and step-mother; (e) mother and step-father; (f) foster parents and (g) other.
5. *Geographical Location*—was determined by urban (50,000 or more population) or rural (under 50,000 in population).

The rate of violent crime was defined as the increase, decrease or stability of violent crimes committed by female juvenile delinquents who participated in this study.

SAMPLE POPULATION

The population for this study included sixty-three female students incarcerated at a juvenile institution. The records of the studied population incarcerated from January 1, 1980 to December 31, 1981 were utilized in this study.

The general hypothesis for this study was H_1 Female juvenile delinquents reared by a traditional mother-father family commit fewer violent crimes than those reared in all other family configurations (i.e., single parents, step-parents, foster parents, etc.).
Other hypotheses were as follows:

1. As the age of the female juvenile delinquent increases, the rate of violent crimes increases.
2. As the educational level of the female delinquent increases, the rate of violent crimes decreases.
3. As the I.Q. of the female juvenile delinquent increases, the rate of violent crimes decreases.
4. As the female juvenile delinquent population in urban areas increases, the rate of violent crimes increases.

FINDINGS

Based upon the collected data and descriptive profile of the female juvenile delinquents in the study the following information was developed. The average age of the female sample was 188.51 months or 15.7 years; the average grade completed was 7.67; and the average I.Q. was 79.29 (see Table I).

As indicated in Table II, 53.968% of the female juvenile delinquents had committed non-violent crimes and 46.032% had committed violent crimes. It was found that 25.4% had completed the eighth grade and 25.4% had completed the ninth grade, with only 7.94% having completed the 10th grade (see Table III). Forty-four percent of the sample were reared by mother only, while only 17.46 percent were reared by father and mother. A point of interest reflected in this data was that 0% of the sample was reared by father and step-mother (see Table IV). The data revealed that 47.62% of

TABLE I

Means and Standard Deviations of Study Participants
With Respect to Age, School Grade and I.Q.

	MEANS	STANDARD DEVIATION
Age (Months)	188.51	18.84
Grade	7.67	1.50
I.Q.	79.29	16.62

TABLE II

Frequency and Percentage of Violent and Non-Violent Crimes
Committed by Participants

	FREQUENCY	PERCENT
Non-Violent	34	53.97
Violent	29	46.03

TABLE III

Frequency and Percentage of Last Grade
Completed by Participants

GRADE COMPLETED	FREQUENCY	PERCENT
3	1	1.59
4	1	1.59
5	2	3.18
6	10	15.87
7	12	19.05
8	16	25.40
9	16	25.40
10	5	7.94

TABLE IV

Frequency and Percentage of Family Structure of Participants

FAMILY STRUCTURE	FREQUENCY	PERCENT
Father and Mother	11	17.46
Mother Only	28	44.44
Father Only	2	3.18
Father and Step-Mother	0	0.00
Mother and Step-Father	9	14.29
Foster Parent	2	3.18
Other	11	17.46

our sample resided in areas under 50,000 population and 52.38%
resided in areas of 50,000 and above in population (see Table V).

Of the sample, 41.27% of the female juvenile delinquents had
committed crime against persons; 38.09% had committed crimes
against property; 7.94% had committed crimes against persons and

TABLE V

Frequency and Percentage of Residence of Participants

RESIDENCE	FREQUENCY	PERCENT
Under 50,000 Population	30	47.62
50,000 and above	33	52.38

property; 1.59% had committed the crime of probation violation; and 11.11% had committed other types of offenses (see Table VI).

The data in Table VII is impressive. However, the general hypothesis is rejected on a purely statistical basis. The data nevertheless, reveals some important findings. The female juvenile delinquent reared in the "mother only" family type home commits approximately twice as many acts of violence as do female juvenile delinquents reared in the "mother and father" family type home. Not reflected in Table VII is the "other" family type category. The reason this data was deleted was because it could not be determined from the records which type(s) of family or other persons were included in this family type category. There were 11 female delinquents from the "other" family type category.

According to the Pearson Product Moment Correlations, (see Table VIII) no statistically significant relationship was found between age and the rate of violent crime committed by female juvenile delinquents in the study at the .05 level (Hypothesis One). However, the finding was approaching statistical significance at the .055 level which reflects a strong potential relationship.

As a result of the data compiled in Table VIII, Hypothesis Two was rejected. Table IX reveals that the average grade completed by females who committed violent crimes was 7.79 and the average grade completed for those who committed non-violent crimes was 7.56.

Hypothesis Three was rejected on the data displayed in Table VIII and Table X. The Pearson Product Moment Correlations revealed -0.16 correlation between I.Q. and the rate of violent crimes committed by the participants (Table VIII). The T-Test in Table X revealed that the average I.Q. for those who committed violent crimes was 76.38 and the average I.Q. for those who committed non-violent crimes was 81.70.

Hypothesis Four was rejected as a result of data depicted in Table V. There was a 52.38% of the female sample which resided in urban

TABLE VI

Frequency and Percentage of Type of Offenses
Committed by Participants

TYPE	FREQUENCY	PERCENT
Against Person	26	41.27
Against Property	24	38.10
Person and Property	5	7.94
Probation Violation	1	1.59
Other	7	11.11

TABLE VII

Mean Violence Rate By Family Type

FAMILY TYPE	N	VIOLENCE %
Mother Only	28	60.7
Father Only	2	50.0
Foster Parents	2	50.0
Mother and Father	11	36.3
Mother and Step-Father	9	33.3

TABLE VIII

Pearson Product Moment Correlations

Correlations Between Violent Crimes Committed
And I.Q., Educational Level, and Age of Participants

VARIABLE	CORRELATION	PROBABILITY
I.Q.	-0.16	.20
Educational Level	0.08	.54
Age	0.24	.055

TABLE IX

T Test - Difference of Means, Standard Deviations and Probability
Between Educational Level and the Commission of Violent and
Non-Violent Crimes of Participants

TYPE	MEAN GRADE LEVEL	STANDARD DEVIATION	PROBABILITY
Violent	7.79	1.40	0.54
Non-Violent	7.56	1.60	

areas as shown on Table V. According to the T Test, as shown in Table XI, 48.4% of urban residences had committed violent crimes, with a probability of 0.69. Table V indicates that 47.62% of the sample resided in rural areas. Table XI revealed that 43.3% who resided in rural areas had committed violent crimes. Therefore, Hypothesis Four was rejected.

CONCLUSIONS

The results of this study revealed no significant relationship between age, educational level, I.Q., family structure, and geographical location and the rate of violent crime committed by female juvenile delinquents incarcerated in the juvenile institution studied. However, there was a tendency for age to possibly influence the rate of violent crimes as evidenced by .0556 statistical significance indicated on the Pearson Product Moment Correlation shown in Table VIII. The data in this study was somewhat in direct opposition with the data of other studies mentioned in the section on review of the literature.

The factors related to female juvenile delinquents reared in "mother only" type homes committing a substantially higher rate of violent crimes when compared to female juvenile delinquents reared

TABLE X

T Test Difference of Means, Standard Deviations and Probability
Between I.Q. and the Commission of Violent and
Non-Violent Crimes of Participants

TYPE	MEAN I.Q.	STANDARD DEVIATION	PROBABILITY
Violent	76.36	15.89	0.21
Non-Violent	81.71	17.05	

TABLE XI

T Test Difference of Means, Standard Deviations and Probability Between
Area of Residence and the Commission of Violent Crimes of Participants

RESIDENCE	% VIOLENT CRIMES	STANDARD DEVIATION	PROBABILITY
50,000 and Over	48.4	0.51	0.69
Under 50,000	43.3	0.50	

in other family type settings needs to be explored in greater depth and across a broader population of female juvenile delinquents.

In view of the findings of this study, it is evident that other factors not researched in this study possibly affected the rate of violent crimes committed by the female juvenile delinquents incarcerated at the juvenile institution studied. Therefore, further research studies in this area are imperative to fully gain an understanding and true perception of female juvenile delinquent behavior and the rate of violent crimes committed by female juvenile delinquents.

REFERENCES

1. Adler, F. *Sisters in crime.* New York: McGraw-Hill, 1975.
2. Arnold, A. *Violence and your child.* Chicago: Henry Regnery and Company, 1969.
3. Barker, G. H. and Adams, W. T. Comparison of the delinquencies of boys and girls. *Journal of Criminal Law, Criminology, and Police Science, 53* (December), 470-75, 1972.
4. Cavan, R. *Juvenile delinquency.* Philadelphia: J. B. Lippincott Company, 1962.
5. Chilton, R. J. Delinquency area research in Baltimore, Detroit, and Indianapolis. *American Sociological Review, 37,* 93-99, 1972.
6. Cortes, J. *Delinquency and crime.* New York: Seminar Press, 1972.
7. Cowie, J., Cowie, V. and Slater, E. *Delinquency in girls.* USA: Humanities Press, 1968.
8. Datesman, S. K. and Sarpitti, F. R. *Women, crime and justice.* New York: Oxford University Press, 1980.
9. Deutsch, A. *Our rejected children.* Boston: Little, Brown and Company, 1950.
10. Eaton, J. and Polk, K. *Measuring delinquency.* Pittsburgh: University of Pittsburgh, 1961.
11. _____. FBI Uniform Crime Reports for the United States, 183, 1976.
12. _____. FBI Uniform Crime Reports for the United States, 180, 1977.
13. Friedman, A. S. and Pollak, O. *Family dynamics and female sexual delinquency.* California: Science and Behavior Books, Inc., 1969.
14. Glueck, S. (ed.). *The Problems of delinquency.* Boston: Houghton Mifflin Co., 1959.
15. Glueck, S. and Glueck, E. T. *Juvenile delinquents grown up.* New York: The Commonwealth Fund, 1940.
16. _____. *After conduct of discharged offenders.* London: Macmillian and Co., 1945.
17. Gold, M. *Delinquent behavior in an American city.* California: Brooks-Cole, 1970.
18. Graham, H. and Gurr, T. (eds.). *Violence in America.* Beverly Hills: Sage Publications, 1979.
19. Griffen, B. and Griffen, C. *Juvenile delinquency in perspective.* New York: Harper and Row, 1978.
20. Hardy, R. E. and Cull, J. G. *Fundamentals of juvenile criminal behavior and drug abuse.* The female delinquent and her behavior. Illinois: Charles C. Thomas Publisher, 1975.
21. Haskell, M. R. and Yablonsky, L. *Juvenile delinquency,* 2nd Edition. Chicago: Rand McNally College Publishing Company, 1978.
22. Johnson, R. *Juvenile delinquency and its origins.* London: Cambridge University Press, 1979.
23. Kassebaum, G. *Delinquency and social policy.* New Jersey: Prentice-Hall, Inc., 1974.

24. Kelly, D. and Schichor, D. *Critical issues in juvenile delinquency.* Lexington, Massachusettes: D. C. Heath and Company, 1980.

25. Kratcoski, P. C. and Kratcoski, L. D. *Juvenile delinquency.* Englewood Cliffs, New Jersey: Prentice-Hall, Inc., 1979.

26. Lander, B. *Juvenile delinquency.* New York: Columbia University Press, 1954.

27. Martin, J. and Fitzpatrick, J. *Delinquent behavior.* New York: Random House, 1966.

28. McCandless, B. R. *Children: Behavior and development* (2nd ed.). New York: Holt, Rinehart and Winston, 1967.

29. Milller, W. B. Violent crimes in city gangs. *Annals of the American Academy of Political and Social Service, 364,* 96-112, 1966.

30. Nye, F. I. *Family relationships and delinquent behavior.* New York: John Wiley and Sons, Inc., 1958.

31. Polansky, N. A. *Social work research.* Chicago: The University of Chicago Press, 1975.

32. Pollak, O. *The criminality of women.* Philadelphia: University of Pennsylvania Press, 1950.

33. Pollak, O. and Friedman, A. S. *Family dynamics and female sexual delinquency.* California: Science and Behavior Books, Inc., 1969.

34. Rosenquist, C. and Megargee, E. *Delinquency in three cultures.* Austin: University of Texas Press, 1969.

35. Runyon, R. and Haber, A. *Fundamentals of behavioral statistics.* Philippines: Addison-Wesley Publishing Co., Inc., 1980.

36. Shaw, C. *Delinquency areas.* Chicago: University of Chicago Press, 1929.

37. Short, J. and Wolfgang, M. (eds.). *Collective violence.* Chicago: Aldine Atherton, Inc., 1972.

38. Shulman, H. *Juvenile delinquency in American society.* New York: Harper and Brothers, 1961.

39. Simon, R. *Women and crime.* Massachusetts: Lexington Books, 1975.

40. Straus, M. and Stunmetz, J. (eds.). *Violence in the family.* New York: Harper and Row, 1974.

41. Tappan, P. *Juvenile delinquency.* New York: McGraw-Hill Book Co., Inc., 1949.

42. Thornburg, H. *Development in adolescence.* Monterey, California: Brooks/Cole Publishing Co., 1975.

43. Toby, J. The differential impact of family disorganization. *American Sociological Review, 22,* 505-512.

44. Turner, F. (ed.). *Social work treatment,* 2nd edition. New York: The Free Press, 1979.

45. Wattenberg, W. and Saunders, F. Sex differences among juvenile offenders. *Sociology and Social Work Research, 39,* 24-31, 1954.

46. Wolfgang, M. and Ferracuti, F. *The subculture of violence.* New York: Barnes & Noble, Inc., 1967.

47. Woodward, M. *Low intelligence and delinquency.* London: ISTD, 1955.

The Psychological Profile of the Female First Offender and the Recidivist: A Comparison

Gary T. Long
Faye E. Sultan
Stephan A. Kiefer
David M. Schrum

ABSTRACT. Sixty-one female inmates of the North Carolina Correctional Center for Women were administered questionnaires measuring sixteen psychological and demographic variables within 72 hours of their admission. The psychological state and background variables of first offenders was compared with that of women who had served previous terms in prison. The psychological states of depression, anxiety and social/emotional adjustment of the two groups were strikingly similar. First offenders were more likely to be married, to have more children, and less likely to have been abused either physically or sexually. The implications of these differences were discussed.

While many investigations have addressed other aspects of female incarceration (Adler, 1981; Fine, 1978; Herman, 1979; Hoffman, 1980; Ketterling, 1970; Lambert, 1976; Sorenson, 1981), little systematic attention has been paid to assessing the inmate's initial adjustment to prison life.

Dr. Gary Long is an Associate Professor in the Department of Psychology at The University of North Carolina at Charlotte. Dr. Faye Sultan is a Lecturer in the Department of Psychology at The University of North Carolina at Charlotte and a consultant to the North Carolina Correctional Center for Women. Mr. Kiefer and Mr. Schrum have Master's Degrees in Psychology and hold positions on the mental health staff at the North Carolina Correctional Center for Women.

Requests for reprints should be sent to: Gary T. Long, PhD, Department of Psychology, The University of North Carolina at Charlotte, Charlotte, NC 28223.

This study was funded by the UNCC Foundation, 1983.

The psychological state of the female recidivist, the woman who has already served at least one prison term, may be presumed to differ from that of the woman entering prison for the first time, but no empirical evidence exists to support this position. While many studies on the recidivism phenomenon among male inmates have been conducted (Bartell & Winfree, 1977; Gendreau et al., 1979; Soothill & Gibbons, 1978; Wilson, 1978), little is known about the emotional condition of the female recidivist as she re-enters prison or about the psychological/environmental factors which have contributed to her re-incarceration.

This comparison between the first offender and the recidivist is the subject of the present investigation. The relative difficulties in adjustment to prison of these two inmate groups were assessed. In addition, it was the goal of the investigators to provide some descriptive data comparing the life situations prior to incarceration of the recidivist with that of the first offender.

METHOD

Subjects

Sixty-one inmates admitted to the North Carolina Correctional Center for Women during July and August, 1983, served as subjects. All women admitted to the facility during these months were asked to voluntarily participate. Over 90% agreed to complete the questionnaires described below. The mean age for subjects was 26.8 years. Thirty-four of the women were non-white and 27 were white. Fifty-two of the 61 subjects were single, divorced, or widowed and 9 were married or in a marriage-like relationship, and 38 have at least one child. Forty-five of the women were first offenders, while 16 had served one or more previous prison sentences.

Measures

Background information. This form includes a total of 13 questions to gather demographic data. Specifically, subjects were asked to respond to questions regarding their age, education, ethnic/racial background, marital status, number of children, employment history, previous prison terms, and history of physical/sexual abuse both as children and as adults.

Beck Depression Inventory (BDI). This 21-item scale (1967) is designed to reflect present mood. The scale is completed by having the subject rate each item according to how s/he feels "right now."

Prison Adjustment Questionnaire (PAQ). This 13-item scale addresses three areas of adjustment to prison life: (1) social/emotional functioning, (2) psychosomatic functioning (physical complaints), and (3) for smokers only, level of smoking.

Spielberger State-Trait Anxiety Scale (1968). This 40-item questionnaire is designed to assess both immediate and long-term levels of anxiety.

Procedure

As part of the treatment program designed to assist inmates in their adjustment to prison, the measures described above were obtained. Sixty-one inmates of the North Carolina Correctional Center for Women completed these questionnaires within 72 hours of their admission to the facility. Subjects were brought to an air-conditioned testing room in groups of 10 to 15 by a psychologist and an inmate consultant. The entire battery of questions required approximately one hour to complete.

RESULTS

Each of the sixteen measures were scored so that analyses of variance could be performed to determine the reliability of the differences found. The significance levels of these analyses are reported in Table 1 for each variable which approached significance. Several of the dimensions have been transformed into percentages to more clearly show the patterns present.

Overall, the similarities between first offenders and recidivists are more striking than the differences. However some differences are notable. The first offender appears to be more likely to be married and to have children. There also appears to be a consistent pattern on the four measures of abuse. The first offender is less likely to have been abused on each dimension. This difference is significant for adult sexual abuse (p < .04).

Both groups are considered at least moderately depressed on the Beck inventory and they are also similar in each of the other measures of psychological state. It seems that, of the measures taken, first offenders and recidivists differ in some demographic variables but not in the psychological variables.

Table 1

A Comparison of Female First Offenders and Recidivists on Sixteen Dimensions

N = 61

	First Offenders	Recidivists	Significance
Age	26.2	28.7	
Grade in School	10.6	11.0	
Married	20%	0%	
Single	42%	75%	
Divorced, Separated or Widowed	38%	25%	
Mean Number of Children	1.79	.75	p<.01
Had a job?	50%	37.5%	
Physically Abused as Child	20.9%	37.5%	p<.20
Sexually Abused as Child	13.6%	25%	p<.30
Physically Abused as Adult	56.8%	62.5%	
Sexually Abused as Adult	13.6%	37.5%	p<.04
Beck Depression Scale	17.7	18.5	
Psychosomatic Symptoms	12.5	12.8	
Social/Emotional Functioning	23.3	24.6	
Speilberger State Anxiety Scale	53.4	52.6	
Speilberger Trait Anxiety Scale	48.3	48.1	

DISCUSSION

Contrary to the suggested hypothesis, striking similarity exists between the recidivist and the first offender, particularly with regard to her psychological state upon entry into the prison. Both the woman entering prison for the first time and the repeat offender are typically experiencing at least a moderate level of depression. Both tend to describe their early discomfort in terms of somatic symptoms rather than emotional distress.

Most interestingly, it is the family history and life experiences of these women which seem to distinguish them. First offenders are more likely to have children and to be married than are recidivists.

Perhaps this greater level of family connectedness and responsibility is an important factor in decreasing the likelihood for repeated criminal activity. Recidivists reported a higher level of physical and sexual abuse both as children and as adults. The connection between a woman's history of abusive experiences and later criminal behavior has already been established in the criminal justice literature (Benward, 1975; Jones, 1980). Many crimes committed by women can be linked directly to such abuse. Further study is certainly vital to assess more clearly the contribution of personal history variables, like those examined here, to a continuing participation by women in criminal activity.

REFERENCES

Adler, F. (ed.) *The incidence of female criminality in the contemporary world.* New York: New York University Press, 1981.

Bartell, T., & Winfree, L. T. Recidivist impacts of differential sentencing practices for burglary offenders. *Criminology,* 1977, *15,* 387-396.

Beck, A. T. *Depression: Clinical, experimental and theoretic aspects.* New York: Harper, 1967.

Benward, J., & Densen-Gerber, J. Incest as a causative factor in antisocial behavior: An exploratory study. *Contemporary Drug Problems,* 1975, Fall, 323-340.

Fine, J. An exploratory study to measure the post release effectiveness of work-training release programs. *Offender Rehabilitation,* 1978, *2,* 215-224.

Gendreau, P., Grant, B. A., & Leipciger, M. Self-esteem, incarceration, and recidivism. *Criminal Justice and Behavior,* 1979, *6*(1), 67-75.

Herman, A. M. If she were a carpenter: Non-traditional apprenticeships for women in prison. *Corrections Today,* 1979, *41,* 24-25.

Hoffman, K. S. Variables relating to program outcomes in a community-based program for women offenders. *Dissertation Abstracts International,* 1980, *40*(11-A), 6016.

Jones, A. *Women who kill.* New York: Holt, Rinehart and Winston, 1980.

Ketterling, M. E. Rehabilitating women in jail. *Journal of Rehabilitation,* 1970, *36,* 36-38.

Lambert, L. R., & Madden, P. G. The adult female offender: The road from institution to community life. *Canadian Journal of Criminology and Corrections,* 1967, *18,* 319-331.

Soothill, K. L., & Gibbons, T. C. N. Recidivism of sexual offenders: A re-appraisal. *British Journal of Criminology,* 1978, *18*(3), 267-276.

Sorenson, V. Educational and vocational needs of women in prison. *Corrections Today,* 1981, *43,* 61-67.

Spielberger, C. D., Gorsuch, R. L., & Lushene, R. E. *The state-trait anxiety inventory. Preliminary test manual for Form X.* Tallahassee, FL: Florida State University, 1968.

Wilson, R. Recidivism: Disappointing numbers. *Corrections Magazine,* 1978, *4*(3), 14-16.

Rape and Racial Patterns

James L. LeBeau

ABSTRACT. According to most studies rape is primarily an intraracial assault. Yet a few studies have found the offense to be primarily interracial. There is general agreement that black offender-white victim is the predominant type of interracial rape. In all, these studies allude to regional and temporal variations in the racial characteristics of rape. In order to determine if there is temporal variation within one city, this study, using police data, examines the racial characteristics of rape for a five year sequential time period in San Diego, California. Furthermore, a factor controlling for the number of rapes committed by the same offender is entered into the analysis.

The results indicate that rape is primarily intraracial during four years, but predominantly interracial during a fifth year. Further variations are revealed when the racial interactions are classified according to the extent of an offender's assaultive activity. The Series offender, one who commits two or more assaults, complicates the relationship between race and rape. The extensive assaults of a few individuals influence the racial characteristics of the crime. The Series assaults of black offenders suggests that interracial rape is not a unitary concept. Furthermore, it is illustrated that failing to control for the activities of the Series offenders distorts the actual number of offenders of any racial group and consequently over- and underestimates the representation of different racial groups.

INTRODUCTION

During the past decade, attempts to describe and explain the relationship between race and rape have received increased attention by scholars. To date, research and theoretical efforts have included de-

---

James L. LeBeau, PhD, is in the Department of Criminology at Indiana State University, Terre Haute, Indiana 47802.

scriptions of the intra- and interracial character of the crime, explanations for the overrepresentation of certain minorities as offenders and victims, and identifications of the methodolgical problems that handicap more definitive explanations of race and crime in general and race and rape in particular.

An overview of previous efforts to identify the racial characteristics of rapists and their victims reveals the complexity of the issue. Results show temporal and regional variations. Moreover, past failures to consider important offender-related characteristics have obscured certain explanations of the nature of the relationship between race and rape.

Do rapes generally occur between offenders and victims of the same race or do they involve offenders and victims of different races? Or, alternatively, is there no pattern? This study reexamines these questions in one city over five sequential time periods. In addition, a factor controlling for the number of rapes committed by the same offender is entered into the analysis and serves to qualify answers to the above questions.

THE INTRARACIAL ASSUMPTION

Menachem Amir's (1971), now classic, intensive analysis of rapes occurring during 1958 and 1960 in Philadelphia examined the interaction between the crime and a host of phenomena. The linkage between race and rape however, was an integral portion of his work. Amir's generalizations and conclusions pertaining to race and rape, as well as to rape in general have been benchmarks for subsequent studies of rape.

Amir analyzed the intraracial character of the offense (i.e., the frequency of victims who were assaulted by offenders of the same race). His analysis of 646 victimizations revealed that 76.9% of the rapes were between blacks and 16.3% of the rapes were between whites. Hence, over 93% of Amir's observations were intraracial. The proportion of interracial rapes, those involving victims and offenders of different races, was comparatively small: 3.3% of the victimizations involved a black offender and a white victim, while 3.6% involved a white offender assaulting a black victim (Amir, 1971,44). It was concluded, from these data, that rape was primarily an intraracial offense involving minorities. Support for Amir's generalizations emerged from other studies based in different cities. The data for some of these studies were based in discrete time intervals, usually a year, while for others, following Amir's example, the data represented aggregated time periods. In 1967, for example, a survey of 17 cities was conducted for the Eisenhower National Commission on the Causes and Prevention of Violence. This National Survey obtained representative samples of police rape reports from each of the 17 cities. The aggregation of the rape information for all the cities supported Amir's findings. Out of 456 rapes, almost 90% were intraracial. Moreover, 60% of the total cases involved black offenders and victims (Mulvihill, Tumin, and Curtis 1969, 209).

Curtis (1974) assembled offender-victim racial interaction data from published studies, unpublished sources, and the 17-city survey. His purpose was to ascertain any trends in the racial characteristics of rape. Curtis was able to discuss six cities which had racial interaction data for at least two discrete time intervals. Five of the six cities satisfied this minimal requirement, while the data for Washington, D.C. consisted of five intervals. Intraracial rape between blacks was the predominant pattern in Chicago, New Orleans, Philadelphia and Washington, D.C. (1974, 26). However, Seattle and San Francisco did not conform to this pattern. In these two cities, the majority of the intraracial rapes were victim interracial rapes. Moreover, of the 305 rapes in Seattle during 1973, 51.8% were of the black offender-white victim variety (1974, 26).

THE WEST PHENOMENON

The higher proportions of black-white interracial rape in Seattle and San Francisco formed the basis for a pattern. Agopian et al. (1974) found that 34.4% of 180 rapes in Oakland, California, during 1971 were of the black offender-white victim variety. Nelson and Amir (1977) found that 60.8% of the 158 rapes reported to the Berkeley, California Police Department between 1968-1970 were of the black offender-white victim variety. The pattern discerned by Curtis (1975) after incorporating the statistics from Seattle, San Francisco, Oakland, and Berkeley, was referred to as the West Phenomenon of black-white rape. Hence, the proportions and racial composition of intraracial and interracial rape were not constant nor ubiquitous throughout the United States, based on the limited geographic coverage of the existing studies. Katz and Mazur (1979) chronicled ten studies of race and rape. Their conclusions support the West Phenomenon. Moreover, the authors include Denver, Colorado in the West by citing two studies that found interracial rape to be 27.3% (MacDonald, 1971) and 40.3% (Hursch and Selkin, 1974).

In a more recent addition to the collection of studies supporting the West Phenomenon, Kline (1981) examined all the rapes reported to the Police Department of Long Beach, California, from 1976 to 1980. Data pertaining to the race of the offender and the victim were available for 1278 (90.7%) of the 1409 cases examined. Black offender-white victim rape comprised 35% (448) of the total (1981, 116).

CHANGES IN INTERRACIAL RAPE

The greater proportion of black-white rapes occurring in the West has been but one issue discussed by scholars. Other observations indicated that nationwide the proportion of black-white rapes has been increasing; the proportion of white offender-black victim rapes has remained unchanged and comparatively rare. This issue has been examined by Curtis (1974), Katz and Mazur (1979) and more recently and extensively by LaFree (1982). LaFree notes that Mulvihill et al. (1969) found the proportions of black-white rape to be 10.5% for 17 cities in 1967. But subsequent studies have not produced proportions below 12.9% (1982, 312). LaFree obtained this conclusion after citing twenty-four different studies of rape either known by the police (case files) or reported by victims in the National Crime Panel (NCP) Victimization Surveys. Furthermore, from these data LaFree calculated an average proportion of black-white rape of 25.8% while the average for white-black rape was 1.45% (1982, 313).

The paucity of white-black events perhaps has been responsible for the absence of adequate explanations for the occurrence of this phenomenon. Generally, it has been assumed that black women do not report rapes by white assailants (Agopian et al., 1974; Brownmiller, 1975; Nelson and Amir, 1975; Curtis, 1976; Katz and Mazur, 1979). However, LaFree takes issue with this assumption because the NCP victimization surveys, which sought to measure the extent of and the reasons for unreported victimizations, showed black-white rapes are more common than white-black rapes (1982, 314).

EXPLANATIONS

Theoretical models for explaining, black-white rape and its apparent increase have been numerous, but two models in particular have received considerable attention. Both models are attributed to Curtis (1975, 1976). Moreover, "both explanations begin with the assumption that America is a highly stratified society with race-specific rules of sexual access" (LaFree, 1982, 314).

One model, the normative or social interaction model, suggests that the increasing liberalization of white women, coupled with an increase in the socio-economic opportunities for the black males lead to an increase in black male-white female social interaction. Therefore, rape is a by-product of increased social interaction. However, LaFree (1982) notes that Curtis does not explain why this model should lead to only increases in black-white rape and not to increases in white-black rape.

The second explanation offered by Curtis is the politicalization or the conflict model. The essence of this model is that black-white rape serves as the black male's mechanism for challenging the authority of white society (LaFree, 1982). In other words, "this argument sees rape of white women as the penultimate way for a black man to serve revenge on his white male oppressor . . . " (Curtis, 1975, 78). A less extreme interpretation by Curtis (1975) maintains that black-white rape results from the black offender's perception of white women as symbols of freedom rather than targets for their revenge.

Curtis (1975) suggested that until adequate data are available, "the wisest course seems to be joint recognition of black politicalization and social interaction" (1975, 81). Recently, LaFree (1982) used NCP victimization data in order to empirically verify the correspondence of black offender-white victim rape with the normative or the conflict model. The former model was not supported while the latter received only partial support. LaFree hypothesized that conflict rapes would be characterized by more violence, personal injury, medical attention and victim resistance. Yet, he found no significant difference between racial groups and the forementioned variables (1982, 323).

NUMERICAL DISTORTION—OFFENDER ACTIVITY

My primary criticism is that the previous works have distorted the number of rape offenders. The authors simply did not control for the number of rapes committed by the same offender. A hypothetical example may clarify this point. Suppose there are ten rapes of white victims; five committed by black assailants and five by white assailants. Hence, rape is 50% intra- or interracial and it normally would be assumed that the representation of each offending race would be the same percentage. Yet, these data can reveal that five of the assaults were committed by five different white offenders; one was attributed to one black offender and four were committed by the same black offender. While rape is still 50% intra- or interracial, the actual number of offenders decreases from ten to seven. Consequently, the proportion of black offenders decreases from 50% to 28.57%, and the white proportion increases from 50% to 71.43%.

This example alludes to another issue pertinent to race and crime. Specifically the overrepresentation of minorities as offenders in comparison to their proportion of the total population. This issue has been examined by others (e.g., Bonger, 1943; Mulvihill et al., 1969; Amir, 1971). In his study of rape, Amir found that minorities were overrepresented as offenders and victims (1971, 43). Obviously agreement with earlier findings that rape is primarily an intraracial offense between minorities explains victim overrepresentation. Offender overrepresentation has been the subject of theoretical debate (see Hindelang, 1978, 93-109) which has evolved into a methodological dilemma (see Pope, 1979, 347-357). While I shall address overrepresentation in my data my main purpose is to illustrate the linkage between offender activity and the total proportion of intra- or interracial rape.

The cause for offender distortion is not intentional on the part of the authors of previous studies. The cause is of a methodological nature in general and of data limitations in particular. For example, the two most popular data bases, the Uniform Crime Reports (UCR) and NCP Victimization Surveys do not in the former and cannot in the latter control for the number of offenses committed by the same offender. I shall assume the authors of studies using other data sources could not obtain an accurate accounting of offender activity or did not consider the issue. Therefore, my hypothetical example and the essense of my argument are based on the assumption that one has a data base that provides a more accurate accounting of offender activity. However, failing to account for the extent of an offender's activity is the major but not the only mode for numerical distortion.

NUMERICAL DISTORTION—RACIAL CONFUSION

Most discussions of the racial character of rape by other authors have concentrated exclusively on the involvement of blacks and whites. While the Spanish-Americans or latinos have received less attention in their roles as victims and offenders. The reasons for this situation are numerous, but two of the major ones are: the non-involvement or relatively minute involvement of latinos; and the preference or bias of authors only to view the racial character of rape in black and white terms.

MacDonald's study in Denver reveals more latino victims (42) than black victims (31) and more latino offenders (86) than blacks (76) (1971, 51, 56). Yet, MacDonald reveals that "three in five negro rapists attacked white women" (1971, 51). Similar detail is absent for the latinos. This is an example of where the magnitude of latino victimization and criminality are greater than blacks, but the author chooses to provide more detail about black involvement.

The rarity of latino involvement was conveyed in Amir's Philadelphia study. Latinos or Puerto Ricans accounted for 10 of 1,292 offenders and 9 to 646 victims. Because of this negligible involvement, Amir places the latino victims and offenders in the white category (1971, 13). Other works illustrate the paucity of latino involvement (e.g., Agopian et al., 1974; Chappell et al., 1971). However, Nelson and Amir (1977) use the latinos in a rather odd manner in their essay on hitchhike rape.

Throughout a majority of Nelson and Amir's essay, even in the section on racial patterns, the only races discussed are black and white—until one reads their discussion of the offenders. The authors gleaned from the literature that aggressive rape is a lower class phenomenon (1977, 286). The authors assert the association between aggressiveness and class explains the large proportion of black hitchhike offenders (21 out of 29 offenders) (1977, 281, 286). Then in an effort to reinforce their assertion, the authors reveal that 4 of 8 or 50% of the white offenders are actually Chicano (1977, 286). It is curious that for a majority of the essay, Nelson and Amir utilize the statistical melting pot by classifying the latinos as white. But when the opportunity arises to characterize hitchhike rape as an aggressive lower class phenomenon—the latinos are conveniently discovered. The authors did not discuss the class origin of the remaining four white offenders nor do they present any additional support for their class labels of the black and latino offenders. Nevertheless, there is a growing body of evidence that suggests the latinos' experience with the criminal justice system is somewhat different from the black experience and greatly different from the white experience (see Bondavalli and Bondavalli, 1981, 49-69). In view of this fact, there appears to be some confusion in classifying the latinos.

This confusion may lead to distorting the actual number of offenders of other racial groups. Hindelang (1978, 105) in discussing some of the measurement problems with the victimization surveys advises that the representation of black offenders may be artificially inflated because some victims, adhere to the popular stereotypes of criminals and may report latino offenders as black offenders (McNeeley and Pope, 1981, 37-41). Sagarin notes that in cases of interracial rape the tendency of people to confuse races is not a myth (1977, 151). This confusion could emerge in police case file data, especially in the cases where the offender has not been apprehended by the police and the only indication of race is the victim's description.

METHODOLOGY

In this study, I present rape offense data from police case file that identify race of the victim and offender and portray the number of offenses committed by each offender. My purposes are to show that: (1) the racial character of rape varies during a five year sequential time period; (2) the racial character of rape varies according to the extent of an offender's activity; and (3) accounting for offenders' activities changes racial group representation.

The data represent all of the rapes and attempted rapes reported to the Police Department of San Diego, California from 1971 to 1975. The total number of cases is 764, but some cases were deleted; 56 or 7.33% of the cases were deleted because they were labeled as unfounded or the elements of rape were not present in the case. Another 96 or 12.57% of the cases were deleted because they were pair or multiple assailant rapes. This exclusion is based on the concept-ual grounds that the motivations for pair or multiple assailant rapes are different from lone or single assailant rapes (Amir, 1971, 182-226; Groth, 1979, 110-117). Hence, this study is based on 612 lone assailant rapes which comprise 80.1% of the total.

The race of the victims and offenders were obtained from incident and investigation reports. Five classifications were encountered: white; black; latino; Indian; and oriental. Indian and oriental were combined to form the classification ''other.'' Using these four racial groups creates four types of intraracial rape and the possibility of twelve types of interracial rape; only ten types appear in the data.

The rape data are presented by year (1971-1975) and are classified according to the number of rapes committed by the same person. Thus, three categories of offender activity are used:

Unknown: The number of rapes committed by the same person are unknown.

Single: An offender committed one rape and is apprehended by the police.

Series: An offender committed two or more rapes before apprehension.

The Unknown group represents the uncleared cases where the description of the offender's race is provided by the victim and/or witnesses, because the offender remains at-large. The Single and Series groups represent a refinement of the cleared cases. The offender's races are substantiated by the victims, witnesses, and criminal justice personnel. The only commonality among the three categories is that the rapes were committed by one person who acted alone and without an accomplice.

Population data for the City of San Diego will be presented later in the text in regards to a discussion of racial group representation. The population data emanate from a special census taken in 1975 under the auspices of the California State Department of Finance and released by the San Diego City Planning Department. These data provide estimates of the racial composition of the city during the final year of the study. Because of the alleged problems of numerical distortion and racial confusion, the Unknown activity group will not be considered in the discussion of racial group representation.

One of the major issues associated with rape has been that many states' rape statutes do not allow the rape victim to enter the criminal justice system totally as a victim, but further complicates her plight and trauma by localizing the cause of the incident within the behavior of the victim. This sad state of affairs was prompted by unrestricted inquiries into the sexual history of the victim. In order to avoid what has been labeled the "degradation ceremony" (Weis and Borges, 1973, 103) many states, including California, sought to revise their rape statutes. The California revision of interest to this study pertains to judges restricting inquiries into the sexual history of the victim and making certain that jurors are not instructed that a victim's sexual history has any bearing on her credibility (see *Deering's California Evidence Codes,* 1978; Sections 782 and 1103). Therefore, the last year of this study, 1975, was the first full calendar year that the new rape statute was in effect. Associations between the new law and the patterns of rape during 1975 will be conveyed.

RESULTS

Table 1 presents the total amount frequencies of reported rape in general and by offender activity groups in particular. The annual totals exhibit data instability. The moderate increase between 1971 and 1972 (11 rapes) is followed by a sharp decline in 1973 (28 rapes). But following 1973, 1974 represents a sharp increase (44 rapes) and 1975 continues this trend of sharp increases with the reporting of another 64 rapes over the 1974 total.

The search for data stability within each offender activity group is futile. Numerically and proportionally the Unknown group is at its lowest during 1971. While the remaining years exhibit only minor numerical and proportionate fluctuation. The incidents committed by the Single group between 1971 and 1974 are numerically and proportionally stable. But 1975 shatters this stability with the number of rapes more than doubling over the previous year (44 to 90). The magnitude of the increase during the same time period that a new rape statute is in effect suggests there is a relationship between the phenomena. The Series group is numerically and proportionally predominant during 1971. For the remaining years this group does not exhibit significant proportional variation but 1973 interrupts any sense of numerical stability with 18 Series rapes.

Table 2 reveals the distribution of racial interactions for

TABLE 1.
Offender Activity: 1971–1975

	Offender Activity			
Year	Unknown	Single	Series	Total
1971	13 (13.8)	36 (38.3)	45 (47.9)	94
1972	41 (39.0)	34 (32.4)	30 (28.6)	105
1973	33 (37.9)	36 (41.4)	18 (20.0)	87
1974	52 (39.7)	44 (33.6)	35 (26.7)	131
1975	62 (31.8)	90 (46.2)	43 (22.1)	195
Total	201	240	171	612

( ) = Percentage Annual Total.

1971-1975. According to these data, intraracial rape is primarily between whites and the predominant type of interracial rape is the black offender-white victim. However, with the exception of 1971, rape is predominantly an intraracial offense. During 1971, interracial is 52.7% of the total incidents with black offender-white victim rapes alone accounting for 40.8% of the total incidents.

During every year, the number of latino offender-white victim rapes exceeds the number of latino intraracial rapes. Similarly with the exception of 1972, the number of black offender-white victims rapes exceeds the number of black intraracial rapes. Therefore, whites are overwhelmingly the predominant victims of interracial rape (217 out 256). White interracial offenders are relatively rare (13 assaults). The number of white victims and the victims of white assailants totals 230 out of 256 interracial assaults. Hence, the

TABLE 2.
Intra and Interracial Rape 1971–1975:
All Activity Groups

Race Offender/Victim	1971	1972	1973	Year 1974	1975	Total
White/White	30	42	35	52	86	245
	(32.3)	(40.4)	(40.7)	(40.0)	(45.0)	(40.56)
Black/Black	12	23	16	21	14	86
	(13.0)	(22.1)	(18.6)	(16)	(7.3)	(14.24)
Latino/Latino	2	2	1	3	6	14
	(2.1)	(1.9)	(1.1)	(2.3)	(3.1)	(2.32)
Other Intraracial		1	1		1	3
		(0.9)	(1.16)		(0.5)	(00.5)
Sub-total Intraracial	44	68	53	76	107	348
	(47.3)	(65.4)	(61.6)	(58.5)	(56.0)	(57.6)
White/Black		1		3		4
		(1.0)		(2.3)		(0.7)
White/Latino	1	2	1	1	4	9
	(1.0)	(2.0)	(1.1)	(0.7)	(2.0)	(1.5)
Black/White	38	19	23	28	45	153
	(40.8)	(18.27)	(26.7)	(21.5)	(23.5)	(25.33)
Black/Latino	6	3	1	3	2	15
	(6.45)	(2.8)	(1.1)	(2.3)	(1.0)	(2.5)
Black/Other				2	2	4
				(1.5)	(1.0)	(0.7)
Latino/White	4	7	6	17	25	59
	(4.3)	(6.7)	(7.0)	(13.0)	(13.0)	(9.7)
Latino/Black		2	1		2	5
		(1.9)	(1.1)		(1.0)	(0.8)
Latino/Other					1	1
					(0.5)	(0.17)
Other/White		1	1		3	5
		(1.0)	(1.1)		(1.5)	(0.83)
Other/Latino		1				1
		(1.0)				(.17)
Sub-total Interracial	49	36	33	54	84	256
	(52.7)	(34.6)	(38.4)	(41.5)	(44.0)	(42.4)
Offender Race Unknown	1	1	1	1	4	8
Total	94	105	87	131	195	612
Total Unknown	93	104	86	130	191	604

Intraracial; Interracial by Year; Chi-Square = 7.41; d.f. 4; $P \leq .20$
( ) = Percentage of Total—Unknown

remaining interracial assaults totalling 26 are minority interracial rapes.

The year-to-year difference of the racial interactions depicted in Table 2 are not significantly different. Only two years are more than 10 percentage points from a median of 50% (1972 and 1973). But the fact that 1971 is primarily interracial indicates the problems of forming generalizations from observing only one year.

Table 3 displays racial interactions for the incidents committed by the Unknown activity group. Again 1971 is the anomaly showing the lowest proportion of intraracial rape (41.7%). But for the remaining four years Unknown intraracial rape is numerically and proportionally stable. Hence the year-to-year differences are not significantly different.

Like the total racial interactions (Table 2), the Unknown group is primarily intraracial between whites and interracial rape is primarily black offenders and white victims. Again, for four out of the five years, the number of black-white assaults exceeds the number of black intraracial assaults. Whites comprise the majority of the victims in the Unknown intra- and interracial assaults. In reality, the Unknown group is probably a combination of Single and Series Offenders.

The racial interactions of the Single Activity group presents a contrast from the Total and Unknown group (Cf, Tables 2, 3, and 4). Every year shows this group as being highly intraracial—at least in excess of 59%. However, the same generalizations persist for a majority of the intraracial rapes are between whites, while the majority of interracial rapes are black offender-white victim (Table 4).

Although the year-to-year differences are not statistically significant some important features of these data need to be examined. Between 1971 and 1974 the number of white and black intraracial rapes are stable and the numeric difference between the two races is slight. This parallelism ends because between 1974 and 1975, the number of white intraracial rapes increase by 30 or 250% while during the same time period black intraracial rape remains a constant 10. The abrupt increase of white intraracial rapes during 1975 disrupts the consistency of the intraracial rape figures across years. This increase suggests a positive association between a particular type of racial interaction within a specific offender group and a revised rape statute.

The racial interactions of the Series Activity group presents a

TABLE 3.
Intra and Interracial Rape:
Unknown Offender Activity

Race Offender/Victim	1971	1972	1973	1974	1975	Total
White/White	4	13	10	17	24	68
	(33.3)	(32.5)	(31.3)	(33.33)	(41.4)	(35.2)
Black/Black		7	8	9	4	28
		(17.5)	(25.0)	(17.65)	(6.9)	(14.5)
Latino/Latino	1	2			2	5
	(8.3)	(5.0)			(3.4)	(2.6)
Other Intra			1			1
			(3.13)			(.5)
Sub-total Intraracial	5	22	19	26	30	102
	(41.7)	(55.0)	(59.6)	(51.0)	(51.7)	(52.9)
White/Black		1		1		2
		(2.5)		(1.9)		(1.0)
White/Latino	1	2	1		2	6
	(8.3)	(5.0)	(3.1)		(3.4)	(3.1)
Black/White	4	12	7	13	16	52
	(33.3)	(30)	(21.8)	(25.5)	(27.6)	(26.9)
Black/Latino		2		3	1	6
		(5.0)		(6.0)	(1.7)	(3.1)
Black/Other				2	1	3
				(3.9)		(1.5)
Latino/White	2		3	6	6	17
	(16.6)		(9.4)	(11.7)	(10.3)	(8.8)
Latino/Black		1	1		1	3
		(2.5)	(3.1)		(1.7)	(1.5)
Latino/Other					1	1
					(1.7)	(0.5)
Other/White			1			1
			(3.1)			(0.5)
Sub-total Interracial	7	18	13	25	28	91
	(58.3)	(45.0)	(40.6)	(49.0)	(48.3)	(47.2)
Offender Race Unknown	1	1	1	1	4	8
Total	13	41	33	52	62	201
Total Unknown	12	40	32	51	58	193

Intraracial; Interracial by Year; Chi-Square = 1.32; d.f. 4; P≤.80
( ) = Percentage of Total—Unknown

TABLE 4.
Intra and Interracial Rape 1971-1975:
Single Activity

Race Offender/Victim	1971	1972	1973	Year 1974	1975	Total
White/White	11 (30.5)	14 (41.2)	15 (41.7)	12 (27.3)	42 (46.7)	94 (39.2)
Black/Black	10 (27.8)	10 (29.4)	8 (22.2)	11 (25.0)	10 (11.1)	49 (20.4)
Latino/Latino	1 (2.8)		1 (2.8)	3 (6.8)	4 (4.4)	9 (3.8)
Other Intraracial		1 (2.9)			1 (1.1)	2 (0.8)
Sub-total Intraracial	22 (61.1)	25 (73.5)	24 (66.7)	26 (59.1)	57 (63.3)	154 (64.2)
White/Black				1 (2.3)		1 (0.4)
White/Latino				1 (2.3)	2 (2.2)	3 (1.3)
Black/White	11 (30.6)	3 (8.8)	10 (27.8)	11 (25.0)	20 (22.2)	55 (22.9)
Black/Latino	1 (2.8)	1 (2.9)	1 (2.8)		1 (1.1)	4 (1.7)
Black/Other					1 (1.1)	1 (0.4)
Latino/White	2 (5.6)	2 (5.9)	1 (2.8)	5 (1.4)	7 (7.8)	17 (7.1)
Latino/Black		1 (2.9)			1 (1.1)	2 (0.8)
Other/White		1 (2.9)			1 (1.1)	2 (0.8)
Other/Latino		1 (2.9)				1 (0.4)
Sub-total Interracial	14 (38.9)	9 (26.5)	12 (33.3)	18 (40.9)	33 (36.7)	86 (35.8)
Total	36	34	36	44	90	240

Intraracial; Interracial by Year; Chi-Square = 2.06; 4 d.f.; P ≤ .80
( ) = Percentage of Annual Total

stark contrast to the stability shown in the Total interactions in general and the Unknown and Single groups in particular (Cf, Tables 2, 3, 4, and 5). The Series data indicates significant proportional differences between intra- and interracial offenders across years. It was previously stated that for the total data set there are four types of intraracial rape and ten types of interracial rape. The Series racial characteristics are much more restricted; there are only two types of intraracial rape and five types of interracial rape.

Like the other offender groups, the majority of the intraracial rapes are between whites. But the majority of the interracial rapes in the Series group are not consistently between black offenders and

TABLE 5.
Intra and Interracial Rape 1971–1975:
Series Activity

Race Offender/Victim	1971	1972	1973	Year 1974	1975	Total
White/White	15	15	10	23	20	83
	(33.3)	(50.0)	(55.6)	(65.7)	(46.5)	(48.0)
Black/Black	2	6		1		9
	(4.4)	(20.0)		(2.9)		(5.3)
Sub-total Intraracial	17	21	10	24	20	92
	(37.8)	(70.0)	(55.6)	(68.6)	(46.5)	(53.8)
White/Black				1		1
				(2.9)		(0.6)
Black/White	23	4	6	4	9	46
	(51.1)	(13.3)	(33.3)	(11.4)	(20.9)	(26.9)
Black/Latino	5					5
	(11.11)					(2.9)
Latino/White		5	2	6	12	25
		(16.7)	(11.1)	(17.1)	(27.9)	(14.6)
Other/White					2	2
					(4.7)	(1.2)
Sub-total Interracial	28	9	8	11	23	79
	(62.2)	(30.0)	(44.4)	(31.4)	(53.5)	(46.2)
Total	45	30	18	35	43	171

Intraracial; Interracial by Year; Chi-Square = 11.82; 4 d.f.; $P \leq .02$
( ) = Percentage of Annual Total

white victims (Table 5). For three of the five years, the latino offender-white victim rape is the predominant type of interracial rape.

In the previous discussions of the racial interactions for all activity groups, 1971 was described as being an anomaly because rape
was primarily an interracial offense (Table 2). During 1971, there
are 38 black-white assaults accounting for 40.8% of the annual total
(Table 2). Four of these assults are from the Unknown group (Table
3); another eleven assaults are from the Single group (Table 4). The
twenty-three black-white series assaults during 1971 is the major
contributor to the higher interracial proportion (Cf, Tables 2 and 5).

Previously, it was determined that the Single group is persistently
and predominantly intraracial (Table 4). The Single group intraracial proportions range from a low of 59.1% (1973) to a high of
73.5% (1972) (Table 4). The average absolute difference between
the annual proportions of intraracial rape is 6.88 percentage points.
In contrast, the proportions of intraracial rape for the Unknown
group are lower; ranging from 41.7% (1971) to a high of 59.4%
(1973) (Table 3). The average absolute difference between the annual proportion of Unknown intraracial rape is 7.98 percentage
points. The Series group exhibits greater variability than the Unknown or Single groups. The lowest intraracial proportion is 37.8%
(1971) and the highest is 70% (1972) (Table 5). However, 1975
records a series intraracial percentage of 46.5. In other words, for
two of the five years, Series rapes are predominantly interracial.
Moreover, the average absolute difference between the annual
proportions of intraracial Series rape is 17.3%, indicating greater
fluctuation than the Unknown or Single groups.

Table 6 is a breakdown of the number and race of Series offenders and their victims. In total, 39 offenders are responsible for 171
rapes. This table illustrates the problems with inferring the number
of offenders of a particular race from the number of incidents or
victimizations. For example, during 1971, there is an equal number
of white and black series offenders. The victimizations would imply
15 white offenders and 30 black offenders. Actually the number of
white offenders is exaggerated by 10 and black offenders by 25.
During 1971, 1972, 1973, and 1975, the number of white and black
series offenders are equal, yet 1971 is the only year where the number of black series victimization exceeds the whites'. Furthermore,
during 1975, there is an equal number of latino Series offenders, but
their activities exceed the blacks. In the Series offenses the majority
of the victims are white. While there is only one more white of-

TABLE 6.
The Series Offenders

Year Offender Race	Number of Series Offenders	Victim Race			Total Victimizations
		White	Black	Latino	
1971					
White	5	15			15
Black	5	23	2	5	30
					45
1972					
White	3	15			15
Black	3	4	6		10
Latino	2	5			5
					30
1973					
White	2	10			10
Black	2	6			6
Latino	1	2			2
					18
1974					
White	3	23	1		24
Black	2	4	1		5
Latino	1	6			6
					35
1975					
White	3	20			20
Black	3	9			9
Latino	3	12			12
Other	1	2			2
					43
Total					
White	16	83	1		84
Black	15	46	9	5	60
Latino	7	25			25
Other	1	2			2
	39	156	10	5	171

fender than black, the whites are responsible for 84 assaults while the blacks are responsible for 60 assaults.

The Single and Series activities equal 411 incidents where an offender was apprehended. Series assaults constitute 41.6% of these incidents. There are 240 Single Activity offenders and 39 Series Offenders which total 279 offenders. Therefore, the Series offenders constitute 22.8% of the offenders, but are responsible for 41.6% of the cleared incidents. Although this finding does not exactly correspond with the findings of Wolfgang, Figlio, and Sellin that a minority of the delinquents commit a majority of the offenses (1972, 88; and see, Hamparian et al., 1978) it does suggest that the Series offenders complicate the racial representation of offenders.

Essentially there are two methods for assessing racial representation. The first method, the more traditional, is simply a tally of the number of incidents by race of the offender. This method assumes that the incidents are independent (Table 7). The second method controls for the activities of the Series offenders by counting only the number of offenders. Thus, in a sense, the Series offenders are counted as if they are Single offenders (Table 8). Because of their rarity the racial classification of "other" has been eliminated from the discussions of racial representation.

According to Table 7 there is a highly significant difference in the proportional changes of racial categories across years. Yet, the only valid generalization emanating from this table is the quantity of assaults attributed to different racial groups varies significantly across years. The actual number of offenders is indicated in Table 8 which controls for the assaults of the Series group. Table 8 indicates there is not a significant difference in the proportional changes across years.

TABLE 7.
Racial Representation Inferred from Incidents

Offender/Race	Year					
	1971	1972	1973	1974	1975	Total
White	26	29	25	38	64	182
	(32.1)	(47.5)	(46.3)	(48.1)	(49.6)	(45.0)
Black	52	24	25	27	41	169
	(64.2)	(39.3)	(46.3)	(34.2)	(31.8)	(41.8)
Latino	3	8	4	14	24	53
	(3.7)	(13.1)	(17.4)	(17.7)	(18.6)	(13.1)
Total	81	61	54	79	129	404

Chi-Square = 29.2; 8 d.f.; P ≤ .001
( ) = Percentage of Annual Total

TABLE 8.
Racial Representation After Controlling for Series Assaults

Offender/Race	1971	1972	1973	1974	1975	Total
White	16	17	17	17	47	114
	(34.8)	(43.6)	(41.5)	(34.0)	(48.5)	(41.8)
Black	27	17	21	24	35	124
	(58.7)	(43.6)	(51.2)	(48.0)	(36.1)	(45.4)
Latino	3	5	3	9	15	35
	(6.5)	(12.8)	(7.3)	(18.0)	(15.5)	(12.8)
Total	46	39	41	50	97	273

Chi-Square = 1032; 8 d.f.; P ≤ .30
( ) = Percentage of Annual Total

Comparing Tables 6, 7 and 8 indicates how the racial group with the most Series incidents overestimates the representation of that particular group; the blacks are overrrepresented during 1971; the whites are overrepresented during 1972 to 1975. The latinos appear to be increasing across years, but one could argue that these data are too unstable.

Assuming racial representation from incident data relays erroneous changes in the number of offenders. The change in black offenders between 1971 and 1972 is not a decrease of 28 offenders as indicated in Table 7, but a decrease of ten as conveyed in Table 8. Furthermore, the increase of black offenders between 1974 and 1975 is not 14 offenders (Table 7) but 11 offenders (Table 8). The incident data could lead one to assume that the white offenders increase by 13 between 1973 and 1974 and by 26 between 1975 and 1975 (Table 7). In reality, the number of white offenders is almost constant between 1971 and 1974. While the actual increase between 1974 and 1975 is 30 offenders (Cf, Tables 7 and 8).

During 1975, coincident with the revised rape statute, the white offenders record their highest proportion of the offender population, while the blacks record their lowest representation (Table 8). However, it is the white offenders that present a more positive association with the revised rape statute. Racial representation from incident data indicate that during 1975 the whites account for 49.6% of the offenders (Table 7). White representation after controlling for the Series group yields a proportion of 48.5% (Table 8). The difference between the two proportions is 1.1 percentage points. Thus, indicating, for the whites during 1975, the two methods for measuring representation are almost congruent. This is because the abrupt increase of white single activity offenders (44) strongly influences the representation (Cf, Table 4, 7, and 8).

The 1975 Special Census counted 770,394 inhabitants of San Diego. The racial composition of the heads of household were 84.3% white, 6.8% black, 6.1% latino, and 2.8% other (San Diego City Planning Department, 1975:1). Comparing the Table 8 with the population data for San Diego indicates during 1975 the whites are underrepresented as offenders; the blacks are almost six times overrepresented as offenders; and the proportion of latino offenders is more than double their proportion of the resident population. Hence, the minorities are overrepresented as rape offenders, while the whites are underrepresented. Regardless, if racial representation is based on incidents (Table 7) or offenders (Table 8). These findings still are true.

DISCUSSION AND CONCLUSIONS

Do rapes occur primarily between offenders and victims of the same race? This was the primary question guiding the research; the answer is a qualified yes. It is qualified because for four of the five years rape was predominantly intraracial. However, Amir's (1971) initial finding cannot be supported by these data since a majority of the intraracial rapes are between whites rather than minorities. This finding combined with the fact that during 1971 rape was primarily interracial between black offenders and white victims coincides with the criteria utilized in the conceptualization of the West Phenomenon by Curtis (1975).

The fact that rape was primarily interracial during 1971 and intraracial for the remaining years alludes to the tenuousness of generalizations formed by observing the racial interactions for only one year. Disaggregating the data and classifying the rapes according to the extent of an offender's activity partially explains why 1971 was an interracial anomaly. Basically the activities of 5 black offenders who assaulted 23 white and 5 latino victims inflated the interracial proportion for that year.

On the whole, the offender activity classification did not simplify the relationship between race and rape, but complicated it. While instability is a property of the data set there are indications that each offender activity group has its individual racial character. The Unknown group is primarily intraracial, but very close to the median; the Single group has almost consistently higher intraracial proportions than the Unknown group; the Series group exhibits radical fluctuations between being predominantly inter- and intraracial. In all three groups, intraracial rape is primarily between whites. In the Unknown and Single groups interracial rape is primarily between black offenders and white victims. While for three of the five years, the predominant type of interracial assault in the Series group is latino offender-white victim.

The racial characteristics of the offender activity groups suggests that interracial rape is not a unitary concept. In light of LaFree's (1982) findings, perhaps we should return to the joint recognition of the social interaction and politicalization models as suggested earlier by Curtis (1975). Perhaps the repeated assaults of white victims by the same minority offender is indicative of the rage and revenge implied by the politicalization or conflict model. The Single group, because by definition, the offender commits one reported rape and then is apprehended by the police suggests the victim is able to relay very tangible information about her assailant to the police (Skogan and Atunes, 1979). This tangible information may be the product of social interaction. Hence one should examine some of the situational variables considered by LaFree (1982) such as victim-offender relationship and the setting of the assault. The hypothesized linkage between social interaction-Single offender rape is very appropriate for Single activity white intraracial rape.

During 1975, with the new rape statute in effect there is a prominent increase in Single activity rapes (Table 1). Moreover, the increase of white intraracial Single activity rapes is the most conspicuous (Table 4). This observation runs counter to Hindelang's assertion that rapes involving black offenders are more likely to be reported than those involving white offenders (1978, 103). Hindelang's statement was not made in reference to social interaction, tangible information, revised statutes, and increased reporting of assaults. Hence, a new path of inquiry would be if revised rape statutes induce the reporting of particular racial interactions. The magnitude of the increase of white Single activity rapes during 1975 suggests a positive relationship with the revised rape statute.

It was demonstrated how inferring racial group representation from incident data can distort the representation of the racial group with the most Series assaults and provide false indicators of trends. Moreover, the Unknown offenses were eliminated from the assessment of representation because of the alleged confusion in properly identifying the races of offenders and the inability to determine the extent of the Unknown offenders' activities. These two limitations serve to complicate the relationship between race and rape.

Rape has been and continues to be one of the most highly emotional and controversial issues facing society. However, the emotion and controversy are accelerated by interracial rape or in the word of Brownmiller:

> no single event ticks off America's political schizophrenia with greater certainty than the case of a black man accused of raping a white woman. Facts are irrelevant to the public imagination. Objectivity is thrown out the window. (1975, 210)

The difference between the assumed and the actual number of offenders may not be significant in an orthodox statistical sense. But given the subjectivity associated with rape, every researcher has the professional responsibility to qualify their measurements of interracial rape—even at the risk of being labeled a quantitative heretic.

REFERENCES

Agopian, M.W., Chappell, D. and Gies G. 1974. Interracial forcible rape in a North American city. In Israel Drapkin and Emiliano Viano (eds.), *Victimology*. Lexington, Mass.: Lexington, pp. 93-102.

Amir, M. 1971. *Patterns in forcible rape*. Chicago: The University of Chicago Press.

Bondavalli. B.J. and Bondavalli B. 1981. Spanish-speaking people and the North American criminal justice system. In R.L. McNeely and Carl E. Pope (eds.), *Race, Crime and Criminal Justice*. Beverly Hills, Calif.: Sage Publications, pp. 49-69.

Bonger, W. 1969. *Race and crime*. Margaret Mathews Hordyk, tr. Montclair, N.J: Patterson Smith.

Brownmiller, S. 1975. *Against our will: Men, women and rape*. New York: Simon and Schuster.

Chappell, D., et al. 1971. Forcible rape: A comparative study of offenses known to police in Boston and Los Angeles. In James Henslin (ed.), *Studies in the Sociology of Sex*. New York: Appleton-Century-Crofts, pp. 169-90.

Curtis, L.A. 1974. *Criminal violence*. Lexington, Mass.: Heath.

———. 1975. *Violence, rape and culture*. Lexington, Mass.: Heath.

———. 1976. Rape, race and culture: Some speculations in search of a theory. In M.J. Walker and S.L. Brodsky (eds.), *Sexual assault*. Lexington, Mass.: Heath. pp. 117-34.

Deering's California Evidence Code. 1978. San Francisco: Bancroft-Whitney Company.

Groth, A.N. 1979. *Men who rape.* New York: Plenum Press.

Hamparian, D.M., Schuster, R. Dinitz, S. and Conrad, J. P. 1978. The violent few: A study of dangerous juvenile offenders. Boston, Mass.: Lexington.

Hursch, C.J., and Selkin, J. 1974. *Rape prevention research report.* Denver: Violence Research Unit, Division of Psychiatric Service, Department of Health and Hospitals (mimeo).

Hindelang, M. 1978. Race and involvement in common law personal crimes: A comparison of three techniques. *American Sociological Review, 43* (February), pp. 93-109.

Katz, S. and Mazur, M. 1979. *Understanding the rape victim: A synthesis of research findings.* New York: John Wiley and Sons.

Klein, R. 1981. An analysis of demographic and selected other factors to the frequency of rape in the city of Long Beach, California 1976-1980. Ed.D. Dissertation Pepperdine University.

LaFree, G.D., 1982. Male power and female victimization: Toward a theory of interracial rape. *American Journal of Sociology, 88* (September), pp. 311-28.

MacDonald, J.M. 1971. *Rape offenders and their victims.* Springfield, Illinois: Charles C. Thomas.

McNeely, R.L. and Pope, C.E. 1981. Socioeconomic and racial issues in the measurement of criminal involvement. In R.L. McNeely and Carl E. Pope (eds). *Race, crime, and criminal justice.* Beverly Hills, California: Sage Publications, pp. 31-47.

Mulvihill, D.J., Tumin, M. and Curtis, L. 1969. *Crimes of violence, a staff report to the National Commission on the Causes and Prevention of Violence.* Washington, D.C.: U.S. Government Printing Office.

Nelson, S. and Amir, M. 1977. The hitchhike victim of rape: A research report. In Duncan Chappell, Robley Geis, and Gilbert Geis (eds.), *Forcible rape: The crime, the victim and the offender.* New York: Columbia University Press, pp. 272-90.

Pope, C.E. 1979. Race and crime revisited. *Crime and Delinquency, 25,* pp. 247-57.

Sagarin, E. 1977. Forcible rape and the problem of the rights of the accused. In Duncan Chappell, Robley Geis, and Gilbert Geis (eds.), *Forcible rape: The crime, the victim, and the offender.* New York: Columbia University Press, pp. 142-60.

San Diego City Planning Department. 1975. A brief statistical analysis of San Diego's people and housing as identified by the 1975 special census. (mimeo).

Skogan, W.G. and Atunes, G.E. 1979. Information, apprehension, and deterrence: Exploring the limits of police productivity. *Journal of Criminal Justice, 7,* pp. 217-41.

Weis, K. and Borges, S.S. 1973. Victimology and rape: The case of the legitimate victim. *Issues in Criminology, 8,* pp. 71-115.

Wolfgang, M.E., Figlio, R.M. and Sellin, T. 1972. *Delinquency in a birth cohort.* Chicago: The University of Chicago Press.

Rape: A Social Perspective

Lynn Reynolds

The 1981 FBI Uniform Crime Report cites sexual assault as not only the most frequently committed crime in America but also the most under-reported. If a reliable count were made the probable total of victims per year would exceed 4,000,000. This paper will examine those societal institutions which serve to promote sexism and powerlessness which are major ingredients in the practice of rape. These institutions include: the family, police and the courts, as well as marriage as an institution of social control. The political implications of research generated from biological/psychological disciplines which focus on individual psychopathology and fail to account for cultural determinants will be considered.

Focusing on the relationship between the incidence of violence and sexual abuse and the relationship between this and the norms prescribing the relationship between men and women allow us to consider these forms of violence not as aberrations but as the result of deep seated normative strain and conflict within the social structure. For example, women are the most likely victims of all forms of physical assault including sexual due not only to their inferior power position within the larger society but due also to their physical size.

Although the legal and civil statutes do not explicitly condone the use of physical force against women, historically, coercive measures have been sanctioned to ensure their subordination in a male dominated society. Thus, the cultural ideals and institutional arrangements within the social systems interact to maintain and promulgate the status quo.

As far back as the fifth century B.C., Cato the Censor spoke: "If you catch your wife in adultery you could put her to death with impunity, she, on her part, would not dare to touch you with her finger. And, it is not right that she should." Even twenty-five hun-

Lynn Reynolds, PhD, is at Fordham University in the Department of Sociology, Bronx, New York 10458.

dred years ago, there was a definite standard which protected the rights and authority of husbands and legitimized the control of women by force. Brownmiller notes that before the Norman Conquest of 1066, the penalty for rape was death and dismemberment but that this pertained exclusively to the man who raped a highborn propertied virgin who lived under the protection of a powerful lord. By the close of the tenth century, the Statutes of Westminster extended the kings' justification to cover forcible rape of married women as well as virgins, with no difference in punishment to offending males. Within the marriage, however, there could be no crime such as rape by a husband, since a wife's consent to her husband was a permanent part of the marriage vows and could not be withdrawn. These laws all reflect a double standard which persists today in favor of the male. Underlying this standard were paternity rights. The husband's authority was considered inviolate theoretically so that no question would arise about the origin of his male children slated to inherit the family name and possessions.

Explanations of sexual assault focusing on individual psychopathology have been generated by the psychiatric institutions. They assume that individuals behave violently due to internal abnormalities, defective characteristics, etc. According to Dr. Groth, who has done extensive research with a population of convicted sexual offenders, the majority of rapists are neither insane nor mentally retarded. In fact the percentage of mental illness among convicted rapists is the same as in the general population. Medical explanations include the abuse of alcohol among rapists as contributory. Groth puts it well: ''Rapists are not over-sexed as drinkers are not over-thirsty.'' Many of these men who become assaultive when drunk are also assaultive when sober. Alcohol acts as a socially acceptable reason for unacceptable behavior. After all, it's easier to admit a drinking problem than a sexual problem. It is another way to shift the responsibility for the behavior to an external agent rather than to the perpetrator. Politically, the implications of research on individual aberrant behavior is to afford buttressing to the societal status quo. If the blame can be shifted solely to the offender or to the victim there is no need to restructure the social system.

Because rape is commonly considered an expression of a sexual need it would follow that remedies which purport to satisfy this ''need'' would be appropriate. Suggested remedies include legalized prostitution as well as the greater availability of pornographic literature. Rape, however, is a sexual expression of power and anger, according to Groth. Rapists say they don't want to "pay for it." They want "to take it." Their interests lie in humiliating and degrading the victim. Rapists do not necessarily suffer from a lack of sexual partners. In Groth's sample of convicted rapists the majority were married at the time of the offense or had readily available sexual partners. Making pornography more available as a way to "drain off" sexual tensions is misdirected for similar reasons, the assumption of the sexual nature of rape. However, pornography by depicting women as seductive, manipulating, and powerful, denotes them as legitimate targets for sexual abuse. If the nature of rape is assumed to be sexual then male domination and submission by the female is "normal." Normal is here construed as statistically frequent. The responsibility for the rapist's behavior is again shifted to the victim. Since if he is sexually aroused she must have stimulated him through her actions, dress, behaviors, etc. Cartoons in the media contribute to the view of rape as natural by portraying men chasing women around desks, etc. The man, usually of higher status than the women, such as a judge, a doctor, her boss, clearly is the pursuer. Not only do these cartoons suggest that trying to force sex on a women is funny, they also exploit the widely held belief that if a man and a woman know each other and/or the man has no weapon the forced sex is not rape.

The cultural myth known as the "just world" phenomenon assumes that things happen to people as a result of orderly and logical processes. And things happen to people as a result of their own efforts. This belief stems from our basic need for control over our lives at all times. This control, of course, is not possible. According to this myth bad things do not happen to good people. Rape somehow should not occur if one takes appropriate precautions. It is difficult to accept that no matter how many restrictions women impose on their own lives rape can not be totally prevented.

According to Beneke it is expected and even praised in the American culture for people to take advantage of each other. Not reading the small print in a legal contract, for example, and later suffering for the lapse is considered bad judgement. And one deserves whatever the consequence. So, if a woman trusts a man and either goes to his apartment or accepts a ride in his car, according to this cultural norm, she is considered a "sucker" if she is raped. He didn't really "rape" her. He merely took advantage of her.

It is useful to compare rape with armed robbery. Armed robbery is no less a crime if the victim is uninjured, according to Beneke.

However, the societal double standard implies that one is somehow to blame for not protecting that which everyone tells you you are supposed to protect. It is important to realize that cooperation in a rape does not in any way imply consent on the part of the victim. Under these circumstances, a victim's fears range from imminent death to retaliation in the future should she survive the attack and decide to prosecute. As recently as 1982, New York legislation was passed which made "earnest resistance" unnecessary for successful prosecution of a rapist. This recognizes that fear can result as much from the threat of violence as from its actualization. Since the primary goal of the victim was to survive and her main need is reassurance of future safety, it is imperative that she be assured she did the "right" thing. After all she lived to tell the story. Her chief fault was that she was there at that moment. The attack was not personal. Further, resistance is a moot question. Although it enhances the victim's credibility no one knows the extent to which it further exposes her to bodily harm.

Another "blame the victim" explanation is that women are innately masochistic. They actually *like* to get raped. They enjoy the pain and humiliation. This particular explanation was garnered from an "understanding" of women's sexuality by male psychiatrists. The data to support this myth was their interpretation of reported rape fantasies by their patients. These sexual fantasies included imagined physical or mental pain as well as expressions of passive desires to be overwhelmed. But the crucial difference between these voluntary fantasies and actual rape is that the woman is in complete control of her fantasy. She is not in control of the rape. If she were it would not be construed as rape! In her fantasies she rarely feels fear but in a real or attempted rape she is not only afraid; she is terrified.

In addition to the psychiatric explanations which focus on the victim's contribution to her own assault, the legal institution tends to personalize the crime of rape. Although rape, like other crimes of violence, is considered a felony it is not viewed as a societal crime. A vigorous prosecution is conducted only if the D.A. is personally outraged. According to Beneke this explains the reaction of the courts when the system fails to protect the victim or convict the rapist. The blame is focused on the victim. For example: "She wasn't credible enough." If the victim is a known prostitute or if she has had prior sexual relations with the assailant her past sexual behavior is admissable evidence for the defense. Underlining the prevalent view of rape as sexual is the sympathy felt for the rapist who apologizes profusely to his victim after he rapes her. This is the occurrence in a majority of rape cases, argues Beneke.

Through sex role socialization, the American family has trained women to need approval from others. Her behavior is guided not from a sense of autonomy but from a fear of rejection or loss of love. Females in this culture are taught the behaviors of compliance and conformity. These behaviors are reinforced by the imposition of physical restrictions whose manifest function is that of safeguarding. The underlying assumption, however, is that females are innately fragile and vulnerable. This belief is strongly held in place by education which deemphasizes physical conditioning for girls but promotes self protection training. The cumulative result of this socialization is not only limiting the field of activity to which the female is exposed but also limiting the opportunities for her growth in self-reliance. For Branden conformity is the acceptance of the world and its prevailing views ready made. A conforming individual bases her self esteem on external approval. She then becomes exactly as all others are and as they expect her to be. However, the price paid for this escape from anxiety and isolation is the renouncing of her autonomous strength and becoming more helpless, powerless, and insecure.

Sex role socialization into conformity and need for approval function to establish the victim role for the woman in social or dating rape which is the most prevalent, yet least reported, form of rape. Her self image as "feminine" which translates into playful, tempting, attractive, unavailable, is called into play. She has been enjoined through socialization against active self-defense as well as against "making a scene." Furthermore, since the conventional stereotype of a rapist is that of an unknown assailant, and this rapist is "known," she does not react to the situation as rape. Even though intercourse without consent is rape.

Since she has internalized the cultural myth that rape is a form of sexual (versus assaultive) behavior as well as her "responsibility" for provocation it then follows that she *should* feel "guilty" as an aftermath of the assault. She *should have* realized he was not "normal." She *shouldn't* have invited him in for a drink. She *must have* unconsciously invited the seduction. And there is no legal distinction between dating rapes and those inflicted by strangers. This is especially true if there's no witness and it's just her word against his. The most common defense used by the rapist is denial or consent. And prior knowledge of the victim, particularly if there was sexual activity in the past, makes a rape in the present difficult to prove. Social outrage is diminished by the preparation and the situation in which the woman has voluntarily placed herself.

Male sex role socialization fosters "dating" rape with the common myth that rape can only be committed by a stranger. So he's not a rapist. Boys are socialized to be "aggressive" in this culture. They are enjoined to "take what you want in this world." They are taught that its all right to "trick" or "seduce" women against their will. And, in fact, it's an admired achievement to do so. Men are socialized to believe that sex is a major need which they must have satisfied by a woman. Upon questioning, many rapists admit that they consider masturbation "sissy" and do not think that "real men" do this form of sexual satisfaction. Since arousal is assumed to demand immediate satisfaction, the myth is fostered that beyond "a certain point" the male is psychologically/physiologically unable to control his response sexually. This fits in with the notion that sexual pleasure makes one helpless, according to Beneke. Note the familiar Hollywood scene in which the heroine resists the kiss of the hero until her resistance turns to the heavy breathing of sexual arousal and pleasure. The "dating" rapist often does not think that this act of rape counted since, if he felt turned on, didn't the victim provoke him?

The notion that a woman's provocation absolves a man of responsibility for his actions can be traced to the objectifying of women in a male oriented society. What is lost is that the man's own perception of her, determined in part by societal standards of female attractiveness, causes his response. Not the object itself (in this case, the woman). However, she is considered a provocation nonetheless. She is then said to provoke her own use. According to Dworkin the object provokes its use even though its form is determined by the one who is provoked. If the object complains about the use to which she is put, she is told not to provoke. Because the value of an object is finally in its violation or destruction, it is no surprise to find that there are men who have sexually objectified the woman who is that violated object. The object must be that which it is supposed to be; its behavior must be appropriate to its function. (This functionalistic view is related to the mechanistic perspective to be referred to below.) A sexual response aroused by an object with specific attributes that in themselves provoke is taken for granted; an objectified response. One of the standards of female beauty is that the woman must conform to the male's definition of her as an object with respect to form as well as function. Female beauty is rewarded. A lack of beauty is punished. But the punishments are understood to be personal misfortunes. They are not seen as systematic, institutional, and historical. Women did not understand that they were also punished through sexual use for being beautiful, according to Dworkin. A dilemma is that women grow up at least unconciously realizing that the way they look gives them a tremendous amount of power. To give up sexism in advertising, for example, a woman might have to confront giving up power to manipulate. Because of her scant supply of power in the other spheres of her activities, the power accorded her by her sexuality becomes over-valued.

The cultural institution known as the dating system in America which places the date in an economic framework in which the male is expected to pay for himself as well as the female fits in with the view of the female as a commodity to be purchased. He then feels he is entitled to a return on his investment. And if a man defines the situation as primarily sexual and seductive rather than rapacious he can call the act seduction. The mythology of rape serves two fundamental functions. It allows the man to both engage in forbidden behavior and to rationalize and justify it after the event.

Because the American culture holds that the female lures the male it then follows that he cannot be held fully responsible for his acts. Thus, the nature of rape is assumed to be sexual rather than assaultive. Forceful domination by the male and submission by the female is deemed normal, acceptable, and usual.

If the rapist is handsome it is commonly assumed that he "didn't need" to rape. But if the victim is attractive it is often said she was "asking for it." Her appearance and behavior are taken as a form of speech. And "actions speak louder than words" is a widely held belief. The woman's actions according to Beneke, (her appearance may be taken as action) are given greater emphasis than her words. Lakoff notes that "appearance as a weapon" theme is part of a more general passive theory of perception. Perception is understood in terms of external stimuli bombarding the senses. Something that happens to me over which I have no choice. But this is not true. Human beings not only actively perceive they also make choices about *what* they perceive. An application of this construct is evidenced by the victim's public response (or lack of) to a rape situation. Thus, the woman, herself, makes the first of many social definitions of rape. After determining that she has, indeed, been raped she then makes the decision to report it or not to report. As the case is processed through the legal system others have the opportunity to validate or discredit her initial decision. Since only those cases that have been validated by the initial phases of the legal system are available for study at later stages, a biased view of the nature of the rape situation is actually presented for inclusion in current literature. Little is known about those encounters that the victim defines as rape but which are never entered in police records.

Sexual politics are the most important factor expressed in rape. The female role teaches the woman to value her sexual favors as an item of exchange in the transaction of the marriage contract. Thus, the woman's worth as a sexual object is protected in the interest of her husband. There is good likelihood that divorce will add to her victimization if she is raped by a stranger (a person other than her husband). She has become defiled. Her value is drastically diminished.

The criminal law defines rape as forcible intercourse with a woman *not* the wife of the offender without the women's consent. Therefore, a man may legally rape his wife. In only eleven of the fifty states can a husband be prosecuted for rape whether married or separated. And New York is not one of them. For the purposes of this law New York is stating the woman is not a female.

The historical foundation of these legal protections of immunity against rape charges can be attributed to the British jurist, Sir Matthew Hale. Hale said two hundred years ago that: "The husband cannot be guilty of rape committed by himself upon his lawful wife, for by their mutual matrimonial consent and contract, the wife hath given up herself in this kind unto her husband, which she cannot retract." The common law doctrine which supports this view is the concept of marital unity. That is a husband and wife are considered one person. But marital rape is like stranger rape in that it is not an act of sexual desire. It is an expression of power and hostility. Men rape their wives to assert power and strength, to punish and degrade, to prove "virility," and to overcome feelings of being unloved. Thus sex is used to fulfill non-sexual emotional needs.

Groth also views rape as sexual behavior in the primary service of non-sexual needs. These needs can be expressed in terms of four basic constructs, according to Groth, they are: status, hostility, control, and dominance. Performing, conquering, and being serviced are all activities that confer superior status. Gaining possession of a valued commodity also gives one status in two ways. One has status over the woman because one possesses her and one is also given status in the eyes of other men. Controlling a woman's behavior, being serviced by a woman, and/or controlling one's own performance all express dominance. To possess a commodity is to dominate it and regarding women as commodities to possess is an act of hostility. In *Metaphors We Live By,* Lakoff and Johnson discuss that the way men talk about sex and women creates self-fulfilling prophecies. Considering women as objects, animals, food, or children is an act of hostility and leads to degradation of their personhood. Further, metaphors may create social realities and thus be a guide for future action. If sex is viewed as a commodity it would follow that the following statements are reflective of that mindset. "I've never had to pay for pussy," "Why should a man rape if he can get it for free?" If sex is considered an achievement the presence of an attractive woman may result in one's feeling like a failure. One's self worth or manhood may become subtly or not so subtly an issue in her presence. And the most likely way to feel towards someone who makes one feel like a failure is to degrade them in return.

It is important to understand that behavior is not inherently deviant or nondeviant. Deviance is a property conferred upon the behavior by individuals in a position to do so. Both attribution and labeling theory suggest that characteristics of the victim and the offender as well as the context within which their interaction occurs becomes intertwined with definitions of deviance. The finding that the victim of rape is considered to be more at fault if she were married or a virgin than if she were a divorcee points up the difficulty of isolating consensual attitudes on the issue of rape. A logical extension of "she asked for it" is that she "wanted it" to happen. If she "wanted it" then "she deserved it" to happen. Therefore, a man is not to be blamed. Second, a mentality exists that a woman who assumes freedoms normally restricted to a man like going out alone at night and is raped in response, is somehow to blame. If a woman walks the streets at night she's leaving a valuable commodity, her body, where it can be taken. If you leave a valued commodity where it can be taken, it's just human nature for men to take it, notes Beneke. After all, if you left your wallet on the street you would be asking for it to get stolen. Remember that men speak of rape as "going out and taking it."

Dworkin notes that neither rape nor prostitution is considered abuse of the female because in both the female is fulfilling her natural function. And one does not violate something for using it for what it is. In fact, rape is incomprehensible as an abuse in the male system as is prostitution held to be voluntary even when the prostitute is hit, threatened, drugged, or locked in. To the extent that rape does exist, however, it would not if females would comply with male sexual demands. It is the female who refuses and then accuses, destroying the natural man who just wants to function in harmony with his authentic sexuality.

According to Dworkin, a woman's effort to stay innocent, her effort to prove innocence, her effort to prove in any instance of sexual use that she was used against her will, is always and unequivocally an effort to prove that she is not a whore. Buying the woman, for Dworkin, is buying pornography. Seeing her is seeing pornography. And being her means being pornography. Pornography, by definition, is the "graphic depiction of whores," i.e., trade in a class of persons who have been systematically denied the rights protected by the First Amendment and the rest of the Bill of Rights. However, the First Amendment protects only those who can exercise the rights that it protects.

The essence of oppression is that one is defined from the outside by those who view themselves as superior by criteria of their own choice. Perhaps it is necessary to understand the changes in world views, stemming from the sixteenth century and continuing on today, in order to comprehend this view of women as objects and as those who deserve to be taken by force. Thus, we argue that it is necessary to get beyond the many middle-range theories that purport to explain abuse and to move to the reexamination of macro theories such as those of Marx, Weber, and others which deal with conflict and power, in order to encompass the historical perspective. We submit that this is one major direction which must be taken in the development of the sociology of violence against women.

For example, Carolyn Merchant, the historian, has identified a transformation in the male view of women and of the natural environment. (Her methodology is related to that of the sociology of knowledge.) The transformation involves a change from an *organic* to a *mechanical* cosmology. She states it well.

> In investigating the roots of our current environmental dilemma and its connections to science, technology, and the economy, we must reexamine the formation of a world view and a science that by reconceptualizing reality as a machine rather

than as a living organism, sanctioned the domination of both nature and women. (Merchant, 1981)

Her argument, which links the feminist movement with the environmental movement, revolves around the metaphor of "mother nature" or "mother earth," the female provider and nurturer, from whom life flows and where in all things are organically united. The abandoning of this traditional organic cosmology has meant the abandonment of the idea of women or nature as nurturing and necessary, in favor of a mechanical view of them both as merely exploitable and expendable commodities; at the service of men as they pursue the goal of domination of nature *and* women in the name of material progress. Or, as Merchant puts it, "the view of both women and nature as psychological and recreational resources for the harried entrepreneur-husband" (Merchant 1981).

Beginning with the scientific revolution, and the growth of mechanics, the earlier vision of the sacred earth and the nurturing female was finally eradicated. Reproduction can take place in test-tubes . . . who needs women? Women were defined as witches, and witches by the tens of thousands were subdued and slain; often in the name of science. It was as though men, through science, could bring nature and the other half of the human race, finally, to heel. It was a time which prompted Machiavelli to say:

> Fortune is the ruler of half of our action. I would compare her to an impetuous river that when turbulent, innundates the plains, casts down trees and buildings, removes earth from this dike and places it on the other . . . for fortune is a woman and it is necessary if you wish to master her, to conquer her by force; and it can be seen that she lets herself be overcome by the bold rather than by those who proceed coldly. (Machiavelli)

He sums it up. See the female pronoun! It is the fault of woman; the chaos of the universe; the chaos of the man; and science will bring it all to heel! It was as if there would be a new order based on science and the new mechanical/functional model; to be applied as *men* saw fit, in their search for Utopia.

All of the questions about male and female as well as human nature, more generally considered, must be assessed at this point. The great sociologists of the past have much to say about the plight of the woman and it is time that this area of sociology be up-dated. We need to look at classical sociology and to the role of women in historical perspective to help us set a course in research and theory building on the nature of abuse in general and sexual abuse in particular. There are no one theory explanations. The phenomenon is as complex as life itself.

REFERENCES

Beneke, T. *Men on rape.* New York: St. Martin's Press, 1982.
Brownmiller, S. *Against our will: Men, women, and rape.* New York: Simon and Shuster, 1975.
Dworkin, A. *Pornography: Men possessing women.* New York: Putnam, 1981.
Groth, A. N. *Men who rape.* New York: Plenum, 1980.
Lakoff, G. and Johnson, M. *Metaphors we live by.* Chicago: University of Chicago Press, 1980.
Machiavelli, N. *The prince.* New York: Oxford, 1935.
Merchant, C. *The death of nature: Women, ecology, and the scientific revolution.* New York: Harper and Row, 1980.
Reynolds, L. Dissertation. *Power and inequality: A case study of abused women.* Fordham University, 1981.
_____. *Wife abuse: A macroview.* Presented at the annual meeting of The New York State Sociological Association, Oswego, New York, 1981.
Ryan, W. *Blaming the victim.* New York: Random House, 1976. Uniform Crime Report, 1981.

Rape as Instrumental Violence:
A Study of Youth Offenders

Shela R. Van Ness

What precipitates the act of rape? Does it generally approximate the rage violence discussed by Mitchell Silverman (1983) and others, or does it have a more instrumental character in most cases? Are acts of rape committed by men with violent careers? As a sociologist employed as a counselor for delinquent teenagers, the opportunity presented itself to investigate answers to these questions. Concerned with recidivism of rape offenders, the Ohio Youth Commission (now Department of Youth Services) was wrestling with the challenge of correcting youthful sex offenders. Survey of the literature indicates a lack of understanding of many basic issues concerning rape.

A random sample of rape and gross sexual imposition cases was drawn from three youth correctional institutions in Ohio. The sample consisted of twenty-nine (29) males with past or current charges of rape or gross sexual imposition involving penetration or attempted sexual penetration of a person against their will. Thirteen cases were charged with rape, and sixteen had been charged with gross sexual imposition even when sexual penetration had occurred. The young men ranged in age from fourteen to nineteen, sixteen were black, twelve were Caucasian and one was Hispanic.

Members of the sample along with twenty-seven other delinquent peers agreed to complete two questionnaire instruments. Only one youth elected not to participate. The non-sex offenders were included in order to allay any singling out or labeling of the rape sample, and to provide a means of comparison of the two groups. They completed a questionnaire prepared by the researcher as well as the Inventory of Anger Communication (IAC) by Bienvenu. Additional

Shela R. Van Ness is a PhD Candidate in Sociology at Kent State University, Kent, OH 44242.

This paper was presented to The Academy of Criminal Justice Sciences 1983 Annual Meeting, San Antonio, Texas, Section on Youth Violence.

background information was then gathered from respondent files. Findings of the study are reported in the pages that follow. Due to the small size of the sample and institutionalized condition of respondents, the findings cannot represent an unbiased, generalizable sample of all youthful rapists in the United States, but the findings probably indicate the types of offender found in Ohio juvenile institutions at this time. By lending some understanding of their situation it is hoped that this information will assist in planning adequate correctional programs for them. Already eight youths in the sample have been involved in more than one rape offense, so the need to intervene in their behavior is important to the community and the youngsters themselves.

ANGER AND RAPE

Feelings of anger are universally experienced, but over time humans develop a variety of strategies for coping with anger within conventionally approved forms. Several questions were included in the questionnaire to determine possible factors which may precipitate acts of rape from the offenders' experience. Only two factors appeared strongly in the data: anger events and chemical abuse prior to the rapes. Typical was the case of Michael, a sixteen year old who argued fiercely with his stepfather, becoming quite angry. He left home, got high on marijuana and hours later raped a teenage girl and robbed her. Twenty-six (90%) youth in the sample indicated they had a fight or argument which upset them between two to six hours before committing the rapes. Their victims were not the persons with whom the fights and arguments took place.

We can only speculate as to the import of these anger-provoking events to the rapes. Only one victim was clearly related to the person with whom the argument took place. Twelve cases involved victims who were not known to their attackers, while in sixteen cases the victims were known to their attackers to at least some extent.

CHEMICAL ABUSE

Following the anger-raising event sixteen (16) of twenty-nine offenders report getting high just prior to committing at least one of their rapes. This represents 55% of the sample. For some at least, the anger-raising event appears to have precipitated a bout of drinking or drug use, but caution must be used in interpreting the meaning and accuracy of the accounts. While some offenders may have become high as preparation for the rape event, others may exaggerate or even fabricate the role of their drug use as an attempt to excuse their participation in the rape. Records were searched for information on drug and alcohol abuse as common behavior. This data indicates that fifteen (52%) of the sample does have a reported problem with chemical abuse. The possibility that at least some rapists use chemicals to prepare for the act of rape is suggested, and deserves fuller investigation.

In response to a question about whether offenders knew in advance that the rape would take place that day, twenty-five answered affirmatively (86%) in regard to their most recent rape. This suggests premeditated planning of the rape event, though on another question, only one respondent admitted to planning the rape event. According to research by Amir (1967), there is evidence that most rapes are planned by the attackers, sometimes several days or even a week before the acts are carried out. The presence of alcohol and drugs was also affirmed in Amir's study of 646 rape cases, where he found that thirty-four percent of the cases involved either the attacker or the victim being on chemicals at the time of the rape.

VICTIMS

In the following table the age and sex of victims in the sample are reported. The unexpected finding is that 32% of the victims were males, mostly young boys. It is uncertain whether this is an artifact of the sample, or evidence of the underrecognition of male rape. There appears to be a need for more serious study of male rape. A record search of the cases failed to identify any offender as homosexual.

Young women and teenage girls comprise the largest category of victims, an expected finding. Weapons were frequently used to coerce victims, with knives and guns being the most common weapons used against female victims in nine rapes. Three male rapes also involved use of knives and a hand gun.

RAPE VICTIMS BY AGE AND SEX

Victim Category	Age Range	No.	%
Adult women	20-24	12	32
Young boys	4-13	10	26
Teenage girls	14-18	8	21

Victim Category	Age Range	No.	%
Young girls	6-13	6	16
Teenage boy	15	1	3
Adult man	20	1	3
		38	100%

(Some rounding error)

More than one offender was involved in two of the male rapes, and five rapes of females.

Violent Careers of Rapists

Does rape represent a unique violent event in the life of offenders or is the act merely one manifestation of violent careers? A search was made of each respondent's social history and court record in agency files to investigate this question. It showed that most of the rapists do use physical violence regularly in their lives. Four or more incidents of aggressive attacks on others were found in the records of twenty-five offenders (86%). Enumeration was done of all incidents where a youth aggressively fought others not out of self defense. Three respondents had two to three violent incidents in their records, and one offender had no history of violence. Clearly most of the rapists have violent careers, in which rape is only one manifestation of their violence.

Anger Control Skill

A longtime family counselor and academic from Louisiana, Dr. Bienvenu developed the Inventory of Anger Communication (IAC), a thirty item questionnaire which differentiates skilled from unskilled subjects in coping with anger. The instrument measures both attitudes and strategies relevant to coping appropriately with anger. Members of the sample completed the IAC so comparison could be made between rape offenders and their other delinquent peers. Did the rapists test as skillfully, as their delinquent peers on anger control skill?

Scores of the two groups are compared in the table below. Many of the non-rapist delinquents also have careers with four or more incidents of violence. There are three categories of scores used on the IAC, a high scoring category which indicates sufficient skill to manage anger in a variety of social relationships; a moderate category involving some skill, but also some difficulty in acting appropriately in some anger-provoking situations. The poor social skill category indicates great likelihood that respondents are unable to manage their anger appropriately in a variety of conflict relationships.

COMPARISON OF ANGER CONTROL SKILL RAPISTS AND NON-RAPISTS

Anger Control Skill Level	Rapists	%	Non-Rapists	%
Good	1	3	4	15
Moderate	10	34	16	59
Poor	18	63	7	26
	29		27	

The findings point out the generally poor level of anger control skill learned by the rapists, with nearly all of them showing some deficit in this aspect of their socialization into adult social roles. This may be a highly significant factor in their deviant behavior, when their scores are compared with non-delinquent samples of students Dr. Bienvenu used to validate the IAC. In his samples, most students scored within the good category. In this study only a minority of both rapists and non-rapist delinquents scored in the good category. If we consider the complexity of normative behavior expected of teenagers in our society it becomes clear that most of the rape sample is unprepared to carry out the type of negotiation and self-control necessary for playing conventional roles successfully. As conflicts arise in everyday life, these youth lack the skill to effectively cope when anger arises. It may be that violent incidents develop when these youth are faced with conflict situations where they lack conventional skill. Use of verbal and physical violence expectedly bring these young people into conflict with authorities.

Why is it that the rapists particularly lack the socialization needed to adequately manage their own anger? Design of the study allowed a comparison to be made of the family income, neighborhood crime rates, and past experiences of respondents with reported intrafamily violence or serious neglect. On family income and neighborhood crime rates, no significant differences were found between rapists and other delinquent peers. Both groups tended to come from lower income families where either public assistance, social security or one laboring salary comprised family income. The majority of cases tend to be from neighborhoods with moderate crime rates. Family income and neighborhood crime rates were not helpful in accounting for the differences between rapists and non-rapists delinquents on anger control skill.

INTRAFAMILY VIOLENCE AND SERIOUS NEGLECT

The childhood experience of living in a home where members fought or abused one another physically, or where courts intervened due to neglect of children, does differentiate the rapists from the other delinquent sample. By counting reported incidents of intrafamily violence or cases where courts intervened in families due to neglect, it was possible to locate twelve rapists (41%) who had experienced intrafamily violence or neglect during their childhood. Only two of those youth scored in the moderate range on the anger control variable, while the remaining ten scored poorly. By comparison, only four (15%) of the non-rapists had reported histories of intrafamily violence/neglect, but all four of those cases scored poorly on the anger control variable. Therefore it appears that intrafamily violence/neglect may be a relevant factor to building violent careers, probably not as a necessary cause, but as a contributing factor. Geis, Kratcoski and others are researching the impact of intrafamily violence on later behavior. This study only provides the clue that a closer look at this factor may be worthwhile in understanding and correcting violent youth.

From the standpoint of basic learning theory, the work of Arthur Staats (1975) is instructive. He points out the importance of early socialization within the family to formation of children's perception of the world and learning. Certainly it is logical to assume that homes characterized by physically abusive relationships would also demonstrate fewer opportunities to learn appropriate social behavior. A number of researchers have noted the generally poor relationships rapists experience in their lives. It is clearly possible that the failure to learn needed anger control skill is an important element in their pattern of failure. More research is needed to define the interface between social skill and quality of relationship experiences.

SOCIAL ROLE FAILURES

The study design allowed measurement of failure experiences in common social roles among the sample. If anger control skill is significant to success in various social roles we would expect to find a greater frequency of failure in these roles among the rapists. Measurement was done by counting the number of times young people's social histories indicated being removed involuntarily from home, community programs, institutions, group homes, jobs and from the community itself for longer than four consecutive days. Thus it was possible to compare scores on this scale for various members of the sample. The findings affirm that the rapists did average more removals or role failures than other delinquent peers. The average rapist experienced five to six failures in various social roles, while delinquent peers, many also having careers of violence, averaged only two such role failures. Further study would be needed to fully explore the significance of role failure as a factor in violent careers, but the findings do suggest that typically rapists experienced a large number of failures in several social roles. Very possibly their failures were underreported in agency files. We must therefore assume that their sense of self involves conscious awareness of great social failure. In terms of Staats' social learning theory work, these young people were accustomed to finding failure in many if not all of their conventional roles. The failure to gain reward in any activity over a long time propels humans away from those roles and activities. For many young people, deviant roles likely contain greater potential for reward than do conventional roles.

ROLE FAILURES OF RAPISTS AND OTHER DELINQUENTS

Frequency of Role Failures	*Rapists*	*%*	*Others*	*%*
1-2	1	3	18	67
3-4	9	31	6	22
5-6	10	34	2	7
7-8	7	24	1	3
9 or more	2	7	0	0
	29		27	

DISCUSSION OF THE FINDINGS

Mitchell Silverman (1983) and Dean and de Bruyn Kops (1982) identify a type of sudden rage based blitz attack of violence. This model is not descriptive of any incidents of rape investigated in this study. All thirty-eight (38) incidents investigated here involved rapes acted out during the course of other crimes (burglary or robbery) or acted out within a few hours of becoming angered by fights or arguments with others. Victims of the rapes were never those with whom rapists fought. Generally victims were less physically powerful than their assailants, and often coerced with knives or handguns. Premeditation of most rape incidents is suggested by the fact that most offenders knowing ahead that the rape would take place that day. For some attackers the use of alcohol or drugs may have been done as preparation for the rapes.

Young women, teenage girls and young boys were most often selected as victims. Males comprised nearly one-third of all victims, though none of the rapists were reportedly considered homosexuals.

The acts of rape represent only one type of violence found in the careers of most rapists in the sample. Eighty percent had four or more violent incidents noted in their files. Only one rapist had no previous history of violence. This suggests that correction of offenders needs to focus on reducing the pattern of violence learned over the years. One clue as to why violent acts are repeated lies in Staats discussion of rewards as the basic motivator of human behavior. Almost any response may take on a meaning of reward for humans. Involvement in violence potentially is quite rewarding in at least these ways: (1) as a means of gaining attention from others; (2) as a way to deny or avoid accountability for one's actions (i.e., the bluff); (3) as a means of forcing property from others; (4) as a way to gain control of situations; (5) as a way to coerce others into doing things against their will; (6) as a way to insult, threaten or otherwise demean the social status of another person; (7) as a way of appearing powerful to an audience, and (8) as a way of increasing distance between oneself and others. Thus from the offender's perception, the act of rape may be seen as useful to accomplishing any of the rewards listed here. This is speculative now, but the possibility of rape as rewarding is clearly possible.

Poor anger control characterized most members of the sample, as did repeated instances of failure in their roles as students, employees, and citizens. Typically rapists averaged six removals from conventional social roles. The findings suggest that the lack of knowledge of anger control skill may contribute to their role failures and violent careers. Inability to negotiate appropriately with others when angry may prove a key factor in violent behavior. Just over forty percent of the sample experienced violence within their family lives, and the modeling of violence may have had a dual effect on their socialization. The violent home has potential to socialize children into the techniques and rationalizations for violent abuse, and likely has poor potential for modeling appropriate anger control behavior.

In *Social Behaviorism* Staats instructs readers on the way humans learn. New behavior begins with simple, brief behaviors which only become complex after repeated modeling and practice. Complex communication and negotiating skills needed for managing conflict in teenage and adult life may in this way be appreciated as very complex, and requiring frequent observation and practice. Further research is needed to fully explore the relationship between abusive families and later behavior of children, but Staats theoretical precepts certainly appear logical to a learning theory explanation. We could then expect to find high rates of social role failures among teenagers from violent families, and the sample supports the expectation. Where family members sometimes settle differences with violence or neglect, it seems unlikely that children could gain sufficient opportunity to learn complex skills needed for negotiating adult social life with others.

Another way of viewing rape and much other violence is that such acts represent relatively simple behaviors more quickly learned than complex social skills. According to Staats, ways of thinking are also learned behaviors. If feelings of anger do motivate rape events then possibly the anger becomes the basis of rationalizing acts of rape and other violence. Buss (1971) discusses the ease with which violence becomes rewarded in our society. Blumenthal (1972) demonstrated the legitimacy many Americans afford instrumental violence as a way to resolve conflicts. It has been shown that only about twenty-five percent (25%) of all rapes reported to police in U.S. society ever result in arrest, while only twenty-nine (29%) percent who stand trial actually receive prison terms (Dean and de Bruyn-Kops, 1982). Is it not apparent that rapists may perceive their violence as rewarding and low in risk?

Blumenthal et al. (1972) defined three general types of violence: expressive violence as a quick physical response to hate, rage or physiological abnormalities; institutionalized violence condoned socially as in some sports and in warfare; and instrumental violence motivated toward gaining some reward. The findings of this study support a definition of rape as instrumental violence. Most offenders knew in advance they would rape. Many became intoxicated and took a weapon or co-offenders to the event. Victims tended to be less powerful adversaries. Review of the records revealed no evidence of brain lesions or psychosis to support any physiological explanation of their behavior. The findings offer directions for further research on these basic aspects of rape.

REFERENCES

Akers, R. L. (1973). *Deviant behavior: A social learning approach.* Belmont, Calif.: Wadsworth Publishing Co.

Amir, M. (1971). *Patterns in forcible rape.* Chicago: University of Chicago Press.

Blumenthal, M. D., Kahn, R., Andrews, F., and Head, K. (1972). *Justifying violence. Attitudes of American men.* Ann Arbor, Mich.: University of Michigan.

Buss, A. H. (1971). Aggression pays. In J. L. Singer (ed.), *The control of aggression and violenced.* New York: Academic Press.

Dean, C. W., and deBruyn, M. (1982). *Kops. The crime and the consequences of rape.* Springfield, Ill.: Charles C. Thomas Publisher.

MacDonald, J. M. (1971). *Rape offenders and their victims.* Springfield, Ill.: Charles C. Thomas, Publisher.

Monahan, J. (1981). *The clinical prediction of violent behavior.* Rockville, Md.: National Institute of Mental Health.

_____. (1979). *Rape victimization in 26 American cities.* L.E.A.A. Analytic Report SD-VAD-6, U.S. Government Printing Office, Washington, D. C.

Silverman, M. (1983). *Towards an integrated theory of violence: Evocation of violent responses.* Paper presented at the Annual Meeting of the American Society of Criminology, Denver, Colorado.

Staats, A. W. (1975). *Social behaviorism.* Homewood, Ill.: The Dorsey Press.

Toch, H. (1969). *Violent men.* Chicago: Aldine Publishing.

U.S. Department of Justice. (June 1980). Rape: Guidelines for a community response. National Institute of Justice Contract No. J-LEAA-013-78.

Walker, M. J., and Brodsky, S. L. (1979). *Sexual assault.* Lexington, Mass.: Lexington Books.

Wolfgang, M., and Ferracuti, F. (1969). *The Subculture of violence.* New York: Tavistock Publications.